By Cliff and Shore

WALKING THE WATERFORD COAST

By Cliff and Shore

WALKING THE WATERFORD COAST

Michael Fewer

Anna Livia Press
Dublin

First published in 1992 by
Anna Livia Press Limited
5 Marine Road
Dún Laoghaire
County Dublin

ISBN: 1 871311 22 5

Typeset by Michael Ward
Cover by Bluett
Cover illustrations by Michael Fewer
Printed by Colour Books Limited

CONTENTS

Introduction   *I*

Acknowledgments   *III*

Youghal Bridge to Ardmore   1

Ardmore to Ring   29

Ring to Dungarvan   50

Dungarvan to Bunmahon   62

Bunmahon to Tramore   80

Tramore to Dunmore East   99

Dunmore East to Cheekpoint   124

Cheekpoint to Waterford Bridge   151

INTRODUCTION

Waterford is famous throughout the world for its fine crystal cut-glass, which first appeared in the late eighteenth century. The place itself, however, is little known outside of the south of Ireland. Those who have had the good fortune to discover the historic town and county tend to keep them to themselves, coveting the unique character of the city, the bustle of the country towns, and the peace and solitude of its mountains and coast.

The story of Waterford parallels closely that of Ireland as a whole, with every epoch of the country's tumultuous history having its reflection in the county's past. Some of the earliest evidence of man's occupation of Ireland was found close to the coast of Waterford, where the dolmens and passage graves of the Neolithic and Bronze Ages are common. Thirty years before St. Patrick brought Christianity to Ireland, there was a thriving Christian community at Ardmore under St. Declan. The influx of Scandinavian blood is represented in the existence of the city of Waterford, in its time the strongest of the Danish settlements in Ireland. Waterford and its people were amongst the first to feel the effects of Norman military might, the county being the backdrop to the most dramatic events of those times. Subsequently, more monarchs, princes and pretenders arrived in or left Ireland through Waterford's harbour than any other place in the country.

The topography of County Waterford includes a rich and diverse collection of features, from the Comeragh Mountains and the rich river valleys, to the long sandy beaches and the high spectacular sea cliffs of its shores, all with a plenitude of wildlife.

A couple of years ago, in preparation for some long distance walking in the Pyrenees, I decided to 'train' by walking some unfrequented route in Ireland. Coastwalking has always interested me; where the land meets the sea there exists a unique kind of

I

world, a zone where the dominance of man gives way to the dominance of nature. Thousands of species of fish, bird, animal and plant thrive in this linear habitat, away from the coastal villages and towns where only the farmer or fisherman are infrequent visitors. I chose the coast of Waterford for this purpose, with a starting point of Youghal bridge on the Blackwater, and finishing at the new Suir bridge in Waterford City. The total distance would work out to be 125 miles. Robert Lloyd Praeger wrote in his book *The Way That I Went*: 'I have lingered over the Waterford coast, because it is known to very few, and is well worthy of being known better. Those who love the maritime scenery of Devonshire will find here an Irish analogue: a high coast – mostly of volcanic rocks it is true, but with Old Red Sandstone at each end – flowery slopes, lofty cliffs and stacks and pinnacled islets with colonies of seabirds of many kinds, as well as Choughs, Peregrins, Raven; and an illimitable sea extending to the southward.'

Since it was not a walk I was likely to do again, I decided to make a record of the journey, and what I found along the way. From the start, my interest in the places I passed through and the necessity to 'get on with it' conflicted, but I found it easy to put less priority on speed. This eventually led to the journey being completed with a variety of companions, in a series of stages, over a period of twenty months.

ACKNOWLEDGMENTS

I would like to express my appreciation to those who helped, in many ways, and made it possible for the project to progress from an embryonic idea to this stage. In particular, thanks to Tom Fewer, Dick Cronin, Jim O'Callaghan, Peter Carroll and Frank Clarke, who were patient and most enjoyable walking companions. Most of all, however, thanks to my wife Teresa, who also walked much of the journey with me, put up with my absences for the rest of the time, gave good critical advice on the manuscript, and was never short of very necessary encouragement. My late father, Thomas M. Fewer, who was a tireless supporter of all that is good in Waterford, would have enjoyed my Waterford walk immensely. Perhaps he did.

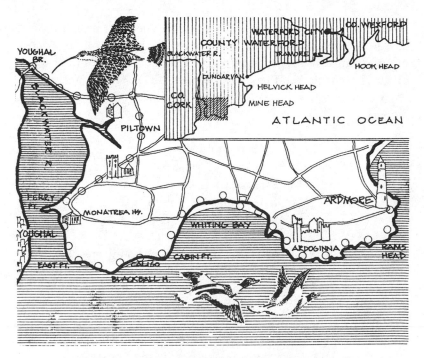

YOUGHAL BRIDGE TO ARDMORE

I could not wait to begin. After the many hours poring over maps and reference books through a long wet city winter, I was finally here at Youghal bridge on the Blackwater river, with 125 miles of coastline before me, laced with a wealth of history, folklore and wildlife. Teresa set off first, striding across the bridge towards County Waterford, enjoying the spring morning sunshine. I tightened up my boots and hurried after her, slinging my knapsack over my shoulder.

Our goal for the day was the village of Ardmore, about thirteen miles away by the coast. It would be a kind of walking 'mystery tour', because, although there were a couple of miles of road to be followed, I knew little of what type of terrain we could expect along the cliffs, and so had no idea how far we would actually get.

A flight of oystercatchers flew upriver towards us as we

1

neared the middle of the bridge. At the very last moment, they divided spectacularly, some flying over the bridge, others swooping underneath. Merging again upstream, their swift wingbeats as one, they wheeled and landed in unison on the river margin.

A plaque mounted at the centre of the bridge has the following legend:

Youghal Bridge
Opened 23 January 1963 by Neil T. Blaney
Minister for Local Government
Engineer W.J.L. O'Connell M.E.
Contractors Braithwaite & Murphy

Before the 1830s there was no bridge crossing the Blackwater south of Cappoquin, fifteen miles inland, leaving substantial areas of land west and east of the river with only a ferry connection. After considerable lobbying by the leading citizens of Counties Waterford and Cork, George IV passed an Act of Parliament in 1828 appointing a commission to arrange the erection of a bridge. The necessary funds were raised, and the Scottish engineer, Alexander Nimmo, was appointed to design the structure.

Nimmo was a most talented man, counting modern languages, astronomy, chemistry and geology amongst his interests, and had as his mentor the great Thomas Telford. He came to Ireland to take up an appointment as Surveyor to the Commissioners for the Reclamation of Bogs, and left a legacy of engineering works, including roads and harbours all over the country. Constructed mainly from memel fir felled in the forests of Lithuania, Nimmo's bridge was 1,787 feet long, straddling 57 piers, and had a toll house on each side of the river.

Opened in 1831, the timber structure rotted so severely that within thirty years the bridge had to be closed for major repairs. For the next fifteen years it was kept cobbled together until a decision was made to build another bridge to take its place. Within fifty years the new bridge was in trouble, unsuitable for the speed and weight of the increasing motor traffic that had appeared in the meantime. In the 1930s most vehicles were banned from using the shaky structure, and those vehicles that were allowed to cross did so by zig-zagging at five mph around barrels. The present bridge has already lasted longer than the first, and looks good for another few years!

Here at Youghal bridge the Blackwater comes to the end of its seventy-five-mile journey to the sea from the mountains bordering Cork and Kerry. For almost fifty miles it flows west to east before turning abruptly right near Cappoquin and heading southwards to the sea. The name Blackwater is comparatively recent, and is the English derivative of the Gaelic Abhann Dubh. The sixteenth-century poet Edmund Spenser, who lived for a while near the Blackwater further upstream, called the river, in his epic poem 'The Faerie Queen',

> Swift Auniduff, which of the Englishman
> Is named Blackwater.

On the west side of the river the steep wooded hill called Rhinecrew came into view as we reached the Waterford shore. On the summit of this hill, long invaded by trees and undergrowth, lies hidden the remains of a substantial complex of buildings established by the Knights Templar. Raymond le Gros, Strongbow's right-hand man and commander of the first Norman foray into Ireland, died here in 1186. His final resting place is said to be the Abbey of St Molanfide a mile or two upstream.

On the east side of the bridge, mirroring Rhinecrew, stands another hill with the musical name of Tinnabinna, whose southern flanks were clothed in a blaze of yellow gorse on the day of our walk. The summit of the hill is crowned by a modern coniferous wood, which conceals a large earthen ringfort. One of the few footpaths or rights-of-way in the locality is shown on the old maps coming across the south side of Tinnabinna and dropping down to the point where the original Youghal bridge reached the Waterford shore. We discovered that this footpath still survived as a forestry track, but resisted the temptation to become distracted from our main goal so early in the day.

A little farther on we came across a neat two-storey house on a picturesque stone pier extending into the river. The house was originally the toll house for Nimmo's ill-fated bridge, and the pier

3

is all that remains of his work here on the Blackwater.

The robust limestone sea wall, downriver from the old bridge, provides a rich habitat for a wide range of lushly blooming plants, wildflowers and mosses. I could recognise only a few varieties, including what I thought was shamrock, but I counted a surprising twenty-two species along a fifty-yard length of this unusual linear herbarium.

After a while the roadside margin we had been following ran out, and we had to walk in single file beside the river wall, into a continuous and frightening stream of high speed traffic. Worst of all were the monster articulated trucks that set up pressure waves as they appeared to hurtle, mountain-like, straight at us.

Ahead of us the road seemed to stretch on endlessly, dead straight for over a mile, but we decided to stick with it as far as Kinsalebeg rather than follow the swampy waters' edge, where the many deep mud-filled inlets would force us into lengthy zig-zagging. To the south, the rounded west side of Blackball Head

4

rose from a glistening sea, but we knew we had a fair distance to cover around the slobs and streams of Kinsalebeg and Piltown before we could enjoy the salty scent of the cliffs.

In the intervals between the howling of passing traffic, we could hear a pheasant squawking from the southern slopes of Tinnabinna, and the eerie call of curlews feeding out on the mud flats, moving swiftly before a rising tide. The expanse of the Blackwater here is a marvellous sight, with the town of Youghal looking medieval on the rising ground of the far bank. A small herd of cattle was lowing noisily in a field inland from the road, waiting to be milked; in their midst a tall *gallan*, or standing stone, rose. I was told when I was young that these were 'scratching stones' put there by the farmers to provide relief for the cows! When I looked recently for more exact information, I was surprised to find how little is actually known about them. Many of them date back to pre-Christian times; some mark burials and have ogham writing on them, while others were probably used for ceremonials and had phallic connotations.

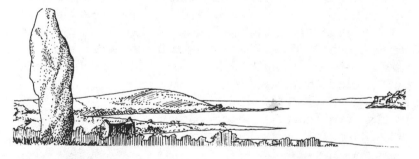

Down near the shore a tall roofless ruin stood — the remains of a substantial brickworks that was worked here in the last century, making building bricks from clay taken from nearby pits.

Almost an hour after leaving County Cork, we finally got off the main road, and turned down a narrow country lane towards the hamlet of Piltown. The first mention of the place I can find referred to the Walshe family building a castle here in the sixteenth century, when the stream which runs into the Blackwater was probably navigable (the Gaelic meaning of Piltown or Baile an Phuill is the Homestead of the River Inlet). Early in the nineteenth century Piltown had a population of over two thousand, and was a hive of activity, when the 'Pill' was harnessed to power a large flour mill, and the brickworks nearby would have been at full production.

The bustle and business of those times are now gone and we found few traces remaining. The ruins of the tiny cottages where the mill-workers lived lined the narrow road, overgrown with a shroud of ivy, elder and brambles. At the end of a terrace I was able to scramble into one of these houses; what remained of the roof timbers and some masonry covered the floor, and an old-fashioned bedstead protruded from the rubble, as if the place had still been furnished when the roof fell in. Only the rich green verdigrised doorknobs had so far survived serious decay. The whole dwelling, which consisted of one room with a fireplace, measured just 10 feet by 10 feet.

Further on we found more cottages, but these were still inhabited and looked very traditional with their half doors and white-washed walls. A bigger two-storey house, which must originally have belonged to the mill manager, is now the local pub. Just beyond the pub, past hedges covered with blue and white blue-bells, we found the decaying ivy-covered remains of the three-storey flour mill. The stream that operated the water wheel still runs under the road and along an overgrown stone-built millrace, but I could find no trace of the great mill wheel itself. A heron sat without moving on a branch overhanging the old millrace, as if overseeing the return of the place to nature.

The church at Piltown is over one hundred and fifty years old but certainly does not look it; someone in the last twenty years gave it an ugly 'modern' gable entrance. I could see no remains of the original church, some stones of which are said to still exist to the south of the 'new' one. I was disappointed to find out later that there is an extensive seventeenth-century graveyard nearby, with a number of Latin inscribed slabs. Beside the church, however, we did find the old 'smithy' marked on the one-inch map, a whitewashed cottage whose thatched roof unfortunately has a meadow of grass growing from it, and a flock of noisy sparrows calling it home.

A little black mongrel leapt out of the hedge beside us to chase excitedly after a passing car. When he decided it had got away, he turned to us, and ran circles around us, barking loudly. A woman came out of a nearby modern bungalow calling 'Danny! Danny' and the dog immediately stopped, and looked at her guiltily.

I asked the woman, who wore an old-fashioned floral and navy-coloured apron, how long the 'smithy' had ceased business, and was told that the last blacksmith had left more than thirty years ago.

'At the moment', she said, 'we have no mass there in the church', in reply to Teresa's comment that she had not far to go to mass.

'The place is in a very bad state with dry rot and they're renovating it. The one in Clashmore was built about the same time and that has dry rot too. They must have had some money that time, to build two churches in one year.'

She told us that the renovation work would cost £180,000 and, while they were saving it, Sunday mass was held in the old hall down the road. Leaving her, I wondered how a small rural community like this, which the EC experts would call an economically deprived locality, would find such money to repair a church.

The local school, one of a standard type built all over the country in the 1950s/60s, looks as if it has not had a coat of paint since the builder left. Opposite the school a limestone cross commemorates, in Gaelic, Seamus Ó Cuain, a nineteen-year-old killed, as the inscription states, 'by the foreigner':

Do Marbhuigeadh le Gallaibh
10 Bealtaine 1921
in aois a 19 mbliana RIP

My one-inch ordnance map showed a well named after the local saint, Bartholomew, near Moord Crossroads, and we were

7

looking forward to a drink from it. Up to some years ago, my research told me, a pattern or festival was held here in honour of St. Bartholomew each year on 24 August, but we were disappointed to find the well obscured under a moss-covered concrete box, beside a muddy stream. A myriad of flies, hovering in a cloud over the crystal clear water, immediately set upon us as we clambered down to the well. Although the water was certainly clean, there were signs that cattle had been drinking there, so to avoid brucellosis we decided to give it a miss.

The salt marshes of the Piltown area are well known among birdwatchers for their wader populations; flocks of up to 700 wigeon have been seen here. It must also be a great area for game shooting: all morning we had been hearing pheasants squawking nearby in the fields, and as we left St. Bartholomew's well we disturbed a large bird that had been walking on the mud flats downstream. It was a brilliant white bird with dark markings which I nearly took for a gannet, but as it turned away, following the course of the stream, I saw that it was a shelduck, one of the more exotic of our ducks which frequent estuaries and sea coasts in late winter and springtime.

At Moord Crossroads the road we were following turned again towards the sea and, although long and boringly straight, we did not mind, knowing it was the last long stretch of road we would have to walk that day. At long last we came to the Blackwater estuary again, where we found a proliferation of mature palm trees and shrubs lining the road, giving the place a Mediterranean air. A relatively modern cottage surrounded by palms had a mysterious pair of cut limestone capitals mounted on the front wall.

It was great to be close to the water again, and look back across the broad expanse of the Blackwater to Youghal bridge which now seemed a long way off. Ahead to the west, Youghal itself looked magnificent, no longer the medieval town it appeared from upstream, but a substantial modern port of considerable character. The fields behind Youghal are said to have been where the first potato crop in Ireland was planted, under the eye of Sir Walter Raleigh, who brought the tuber from the New World and for a while was Mayor of Youghal.

We took a short detour to have a look at the old Protestant Parish church of Kinsalebeg, erected in 1821 but, like many more in the Irish countryside, now in ruins. As we entered a field to cross to the church, a merlin darted out of the hedge and, instead of fleeing, glided jerkily over to give us the once over. Coming to within six feet of us at shoulder level, it banked slightly, showing its underside like an aircraft performing at an airshow, and with a couple of strong unhurried wingbeats, disappeared through the hedge into the next field.

The churchyard was overgrown, full of vicious nettles which left their mark on both of us. The walls of the roofless church were in perfect order with no sign of cracks, the windows sandstone-lined and gothic-arched, with red brick relieving arches. Only this brickwork showed wear and tear, and its subsidence eventually will weaken the walls. The main doorway was spanned by an unusual ogee arch, a strangely eastern-looking feature.

Returning to the road, after a short distance we came upon the answer to the mystery of the stone capitals seen earlier. The remains of an elaborate mansion of former days, two wings of which were roofless, had what appeared to be a typical Georgian farmhouse growing out of its middle. The windows in the ruined section were wide and tall and framed with beautifully cut limestone Ionic pilasters, some without capitals. Although this house was not named on my one-inch maps, I suspect it might be the Prospect Hall shown on Charles Smith's map of 1746.

Not far from Prospect Hall, before the coast turns south for the open sea, a spit of land extends like a finger out across the Blackwater towards Youghal. Called the Ferry Point, it was here that the river was crossed before the bridge upstream was built. Although there must be some good reason, it is difficult to figure out why the original bridge was not constructed here. Maybe its closeness to the sea and the low-lying nature of the spit had something to do with it; even on a warm calm day, the picturesque whitewashed cottage, sited at the tip of the point, looked to be in a very vulnerable position in relation to breakers rolling in from the open sea.

It is said that this spit of land was once of considerably greater extent, and had a substantial rabbit warren in the Middle Ages, when the animals were bred for food and furs.

At the Ferry Point we finally left the hard tarmac on which we had been walking for nearly two hours. Turning towards the open sea, we crossed an area of spongy grass and, passing through a chevaux- de-frise of plastic bottles, made our way to a stoney beach that stretched out past Monatrea House towards the cliffs. The tide was high by now, so there was no way we could pass by Monatrea other than along the top of the fifteen-foot sea wall that contains the meadow at the front of the house. Not wanting to trespass, we did this quietly and quickly, but anyone looking out to sea from the house must have wondered about this strange pair trotting along the top of the wall and disappearing into the bushes further on! Monatrea was built in the early eighteenth century by the Reverend Percy Scott Smith. He married one of the Odell family of Ardmore, who owned most of the land in this area. The house is much larger than it initially appears; it must have looked very modern, with its low-pitched roof, when it was built.

We climbed down from the wall at the seaward end of the Monstrea demesne and within minutes were enjoying the luxury of walking in grass, following a faint track through the fields. The cliffs increased in height steadily and the salt sea smell strengthened as we headed out towards Blackball Head. We were probably the first of the season to follow the cliff path, and the gorse and new growth brambles made our progress painful in places. Having taken the path for granted, we were disappointed to find that it sometimes disappeared, and we had to beat a way through solid brush with our trusty walking sticks.

However the rewards were great for all our breathless sweaty hacking and stinging legs; rounding East Point we saw Blackball Head shelving into the sea before us, and to the west an extensive and unusual view of Youghal. Knockadoon Head was visible down the Cork coast through the haze, with Cable Island unmistakable offshore. Youghal beach was a great white expanse extending westwards from the southern end of the town, stitched with the stumps of timber breakwaters. Not very deep beneath the sand there is a foundation of peat, indicating that the land

mass in this area extended further out to sea in prehistoric times. During the last century, peat was extracted from under the sand for fuel, and during the course of this work perfectly preserved trees complete with leaves were found, in addition to assorted animal bones and the antlers of a Great Irish Deer.

The first real beach we came upon nestled in Mangan's Bay, just west of Blackball Head. It is a secluded beach, shared by two nicely sited and well-kept bungalows; the reason for the seclusion may be the five strand barbed-wire fence crossing the rough path into the cove. We negotiated this, the first serious fence we had met, without too much difficulty, but then had to make our way inland through a field and a spotless farmyard before we could turn back towards the sea.

Out onto Blackball Head we trekked, with a pair of stonechats following and rasping their disapproval from the gorse bushes. The cliffs extended in ragged rocks into the sea, their grassy edges laced with sea-pinks and bladder campion. A kestrel with white cheeks and pointed wings rose screeching in front of us, and furiously circled, bombarding us with its piercing cry. I assumed that its mate was on the nest we had unknowingly approached, and it was putting up a diversionary show.

The sweet and heady scent of wildflowers and herbs flavouring the clean salt air of Blackball Head was very welcome after our time on the road. Rounding the head, Ardoginna Point came into view across the far side of Whiting Bay, the ruins of Ardoginna House making strange gothic shapes on the skyline. Here in Caliso Bay, the cliffs drop down to meet a fine sandy beach a few hundred yards long. I was disappointed to find out later that Caliso is not pronounced 'Cal-lie-sow', but 'Cal-iss-o', sounding more like callouses than Calypsos! As we descended the grassy slopes towards the beach, a rock pipit flew up inches in front of my foot, just stopping me from stepping on its nest, tucked under a tuft of grass, complete with three blue-green eggs. We clambered down some craggy rocks onto the sand without much difficulty, and disturbed a dozen shelducks, who took off in perfect formation – a beautiful sight.

It was now one o'clock and since we were in sight of Ardoginna, which in turn is not far from Ardmore, we decided to have lunch. It would have been difficult to find a better place to eat; the air was cool near the water after the heat of tramping along the cliffs, and we enjoyed being still awhile as we drank our coffee, listening to the rustle of the gravel being rolled by the wavelets.

Caliso is a stoney, sandy beach with an air of remoteness. A few small houses, one of them a thatched cottage, overlook the sea from behind the beach. One of the indications of the unfrequented nature of the beach was the visual richness of the pebbles that cover it and the number of exotically coloured minerals per square metre. I have found that, despite having limitless numbers of pebbles, beaches which cater for people in large numbers never have the density of treasures found on lesser frequented beaches. Indeed, I find it difficult to resist stones of colour purity, fine shape, or with natural decorative features, and I can often come back from a short walk on a beach with pockets bulging with riches!

As we ascended the steep grassy cliff to Cabin Point, the westerly portal of Whiting Bay, a lone chough put on a fabulous aerial display for us. First the phenomenal characteristic roller-coaster flight was demonstrated, up and down at breakneck speed along the cliff edge, then snapping his wings into a completely different square shape and hurtling down the cliff face into a nearby cove.

In moments he reappeared to circle us and watch, quite unafraid. Coming very close, his spread wings, with splayed finger-like tips, caught the sea breeze. Like the hawk earlier in the day, he may have been on sentry duty while his mate was sitting on a nest below the cliff-top.

East of Caliso Bay sturdy stiles are provided for those crossing the fences and ditches, a most civilised arrangement. As we rounded Cabin Point the great expanse of Whiting Bay was laid out before us, a black seaweed-covered field of rock dividing the long sandy beach in two. The clay cliffs at the back of the strand drop down to allow a stream to enter the sea, and then rise up again towards Ardoginna Point, the eastern portal of the bay.

Tradition has it that centuries ago the Blackwater divided at Piltown, flowing into the sea here as well as at Youghal, making an island of the high ground behind Blackball Head. There is certainly a low-lying neck of fertile alluvial land that runs back to Piltown, and the Irish name for the strand and hinterland at Whiting Bay is Beal Abha or 'river mouth'. Another proof offered for the hypothesis is that Youghal is a relatively new town, while Ardmore's importance in ancient times may be partly due to its position near a great river mouth.

The track widened out into a boreen as we headed up between ditches laden with a rich variety of herbs and white bluebells and past a picturesque terrace of old cottages, which were once the homes of the coastguards that watched this bay. On my map a holy well called Tobar Tobachta was shown nearby, and we decided to see if it was still there.

We met a thickset man with a weatherbeaten face coming along the boreen and asked him if the holy well was nearby.

'Just up the hill there.'

'Is it alright to drink out of it?' Teresa asked.

'Oh, it is yeh' he replied, looking us up and down.

'Is it a cure for anything in particular?' she asked, beginning to think he was a man of little words.

'I never heard it was, no I can't say!' he laughed.

'Do you live here?' I asked, throwing all caution to the wind.

'Oh, I do, just there,' he said, pointing to a cottage and went on to talk about the other houses.

'Those houses were coastguard houses, going back a long time. There were coastguards all along the coast years ago. I never heard much history,' he seemed to apologise, 'I don't know much about it, but I'd like to find out something about it, I would. They're all bought up now but the one, for holiday houses.'

'It's no wonder; it's a lovely place. It must be a big farmer that owns that wheat field,' I said, pointing to the expanse of crops on the flat prairie inland from the cliffs, acres and acres of sprouting wheat.

'You're right, but 'tis going all the time, the land,' the man said. 'Into the sea it's going. Over along there you can see a line of pipes sticking out of the cliffs; that's a road that's disappeared. There's houses gone as well. It's going all the time, here in Whiting Bay more than anywhere else.'

'What do you think of the stories that the Blackwater used to flow out through the bay here?'

'They do say that, don't they, but sure the thing is, what happened then? How did it go? How did it change? I often heard it said alright. There were houses and all at Whiting Bay that are long gone, there's no protection at all from the sea here. Will I get a cup for you to take the water?'

We thanked him and said we had cups in our knapsacks, so he wished us well and went off downhill as we walked up the boreen to the well. On the way we passed his cottage. It was beautifully kept, the path leading to the front door flanked by two small lawns on which stood a marvellous collection of artefacts, a private folk museum with everything from an old mechanical fire bellows to mangles, grinders and horse-drawn ploughs. On a shed at the side hung a lifebelt with the name Samson on it; from a craneship which had been the centre of a controversy when it was driven onto the rocks near Ram's Head in 1988.

Tobar Tobachta is in perfect condition, recently whitewashed, and producing a prodigious flow of water. Someone, probably our friend again, had arranged a pipe which allowed the overflow to cascade into a roadside drain. A white enamelled basin stood near the cascade, with the peelings of a feed of parsnips in it, so the well had temporal as well as spiritual uses! Although I could not find any saint's name associated with this well, I have read that it was used for penitential rights, and the Waterford historian Canon Power wrote that a pattern was still going on here at the turn of the twentieth century. We found the waters cool, sweet-tasting and most refreshing.

After a short rest at the well, we set off across the boulderclay cliffs that back Whiting Bay. For the first time since leaving the Blackwater estuary, we could see for a long way inland again, up along the valley towards Piltown, and in the distance to the north I could see the blue rounded shape of the Knockmealdown mountains.

Towards the middle of the bay we found we were walking over a field where many acres of carrots had been planted and apparently failed. The sandy soil was full of them, their rotting tops protruding from the ground, many of them half-eaten by rabbits and birds. Suddenly the coastal erosion that the man back at the well had been talking about became very clear when the path we were following disappeared over the edge of the cliff. The ragged and raw condition of the cliff edge suggested that it could not have happened more than a few days before.

15

A bit more than halfway around the bay we came to a ruined house that might in better days have been Grange House, which a nineteenth-century guide refers to as 'a bathing establishment of Sir Richard Musgrove, one of the best of Irishmen'. It had signs of having been used recently by someone with agricultural ideas. At the back of the house the stone-built 'out-offices' had been neatly refurbished, and the courtyard surrounded by these buildings had been cobbled and planted with a large number of daffodils and young trees. Everything, however, had the sad look of having been recently abandoned, a kind of agri *Marie Celeste*, and all the crops surrounding the building looked as if they had failed dismally.

Near the ruined house, the public road comes to the beach at a gravelled and untidy car park, where we found a man walking a fine thoroughbred racehorse in wide circles. When I asked him about Grange House, he did not know the name, but he told me that the crossroads just a short distance inland was called Grange.

I was following him around in the circle as we talked, and he said, 'I'm drying out the mare after she's had a good run, so I'm sorry I can't stop. Her name's Diana's Daughter, and she's done well in a few outings lately. We have high hopes for her in the point to point on Sunday.'

I asked him why he did not just take the horse for a walk.

'I don't know really,' he said; 'we always take them round in circles. If you see the marks of a ring on the ground around these parts, it's either the fairies or a good horse.' He laughed.

We wished him and Diana's Daughter luck and made our way down onto the beach. It was a fine extent of sand with the tide out, about half-a-mile long, and probably terrific for surfing. I was puzzled by a number of large slabs of seaweed-covered rock occupying the middle of the beach: they looked entirely out of character with the geology of the area and yet it was doubtful if they were erratics dropped by an Ice Age glacier. On closer examination the mystery was quickly solved. What we were looking at was the remains of a concrete bridge that had crossed the stream running onto the strand nearby, broken and scattered like Lego blocks by the awesome power of the sea. Of the road that led to the bridge there was no trace.

Leaving the beach, we climbed the springy turf of the low cliffs bordering the eastern end of the bay. As we went, the wind began to stir, the sea changed colour from a friendly blue to a not-so-friendly grey and we felt the temperature drop. It was after three o'clock and the best of the day had gone.

Crossing a small headland we came upon another beach, this one smaller and more sheltered, enclosed by ancient cliffs which seemed to be prevented from collapsing onto the sand by astonishing buttress-like arches. So perfect were the rounded slices of stone that made up these arches, that later in Ardmore it was difficult to resist considering the possibility that the stones that were used to construct the round tower were taken from here. Under the natural arches, caves extended for a considerable distance under the cliffs.

Near the beach are the ruins of an old lime kiln, where limestone, delivered by boat from quarries like Ballinacourty near Dungarvan, was processed for fertiliser. Kilns of this kind were probably introduced here by the Normans, when they were mainly used for the production of lime for building. In the eighteenth century, when organised agriculture became intensive in Ireland, it was common to use lime together with animal and human dung to improve the soil. In coastal areas it was an economic proposition to ship large quantities of the rock by boat, and process it near the shore. Kilns like the one here were built along the coast, and operated continuously, the broken stone being fed into the top of the kiln in alternate layers with fuel, and the resulting quicklime drawn off from the bottom. As well as being used on the land, lime mixed with water was the material used to whitewash the workers' cottages, giving at once a bright clean finish and an additional layer of waterproofing to the mud walls. It was a tradition in the countryside to whitewash once a year, so one can almost tell the age of a mud-walled cottage by the thickness of the whitewash layer. During the nineteenth century the costs of shipping the stone increased, while the cost of other more immediately effective fertilisers like guano became cheaper, and the kilns fell into disuse.

Up along the cliffs it was an interesting pastime to try to match the ravines and promontories with the names on my map; every

little feature along here seems to have a name, most of them referring to animals or birds. While dogs, cats, goats, sheep, cows,
foxes and rams get an honourable mention, as do all the birds of
the coast, the only animal we spotted between Whiting Bay and
Ardmore was a lone seal, head upright and steady as a rock in the
churning foam below.

At Ardoginna Point we turned inland to look over the ruins of
Ardoginna House, whose towers and belfry had been presenting
a most dramatic and unusual silhouette on our skyline all afternoon. The ruins stand in a dip in the land about half-a-mile from
the cliffs, a fairytale cluster of castellated walls and towers, the
main one of which is an Italianate structure of brick and stone,
forty feet high. The walls are clothed in thick ivy, which in some
places has been sculpted by the salt sea winds into grotesque,
nightmarish shapes. The roofs are long gone, although some of
the gothic arched windows still have their shutters, squeaking
back and forth in the wind. It is an eerie place.

In pre-Cromwellian times the lands around Ardoginna were
owned by the Geraldines of Dromana, but they were dispossessed
and sent to Connaught in 1654. On the accession of Charles II, Sir
James Fitzgerald was back from his enforced exile in the west, but
the lands were again confiscated in 1691.

When the sale by 'cant' (the local word for auction) of
Forfeited Estates took place in 1702, Ardoginna and a further
£5,000 worth of lands in County Waterford were bought by Sir
Thomas Prendergast, who built a house at Ardoginna.
Prendergast was a tough landlord and had a Hellfire Club reputation for mistreating his servants. On one occasion he is said to
have hanged one of his retainers from his dining room ceiling,
and had the body buried under the kitchen floor. The skeleton
was discovered when building works were going on many years
later.

By 1710 Prendergast had moved on, selling his lands to a
family from Youghal called Coughlan. The Coughlans were never
particularly well off, and towards the end of the eighteenth century they were possibly involved in the smuggling trade.
Smuggling was a popular and not entirely unrespectable activity
at the time, and in the 1780s illicit trade was so prevalent in this

area that it nearly put the port of Youghal out of business. To counteract the threat, preventative officers were stationed at various points along the coast to watch out for and arrest smugglers, but of course it was impossible to police every cove twenty-four hours a day.

Ardoginna House, isolated and remote, would have been ideally placed for the Coughlans to take a part in the trade, but records show that John Coughlan of Ardoginna was appointed as a preventative officer in 1788 at a salary of £50 per annum.

There were three particularly beautiful girls in the Coughlan family, and although the family were quite poor, the girls never failed to turn up at house parties or dances in nearby Youghal in anything but brand new silk dresses, difficult to provide on a preventative officer's salary.

The eldest girl, Anne, married Lord Barrymore, Earl of Cork and drinking and gambling companion of the Prince Regent. She brought her sister Elizabeth to London, and she captured the heart of the exiled French count, Edmund Charles de la Croix, Comte de Castries. They soon married and when things quietened down in Paris, after the Revolution, they moved to the Count's house in Faubourg St. Germain. Elizabeth quickly settled down to being a Comtesse during a constant round of social engagements, one of which was the coronation of Louis XVIII.

Meanwhile, the third daughter of the Coughlan clan married into one of the wealthiest families in the British Isles and became the Countess of Llandaff. So from this humble and isolated house on the Waterford coast, new blood was introduced into the aristocracy of Europe.

It is probable that the exotic ruins that can be seen today are the result of a reconstruction of the house that took place about 1832, when the property had passed into the ownership of the Comte de Castries. Four hundred acres of mediocre land in Ireland could not have meant much, however, to a member of the French aristocracy, particularly during the ravages of the Famine, when there could have been little revenue from the property, and Ardoginna was sold in the 1860s to Sir Joseph McKenna, the local MP. He died in 1906 and his mausoleum can be found a few hundred yards from the house sporting angels and quotations from

19

Shakespeare and Tennyson. Since World War I the buildings have become ruined, but their unusual and gothic forms never fail to attract the attention of curious passers-by.

There is an interesting footnote to the Ardoginna story. In 1859 Marie Edme MacMahon, a descendant of one of the Wild Geese, commanded the French and Sardinian armies that defeated the Austrians at the Battle of Magenta in Northern Italy, and as a reward was promoted to Marshal, and created Duc de Magenta by Napoleon III. In 1870, after a brief imprisonment following the Franco-Prussian War, he was instrumental in putting down the Paris Commune, which led to his being elected President of the Third Republic. Marshal MacMahon's wife was the grand-daughter of Elizabeth Coughlan.

Leaving Ardoginna, we followed a dilapidated stone wall that defends fields of nitrogen-enriched grass from the gorse that thickly cloaks the cliff top, until we were forced inland by a deep, steep-sided ravine called Gleann Piarais. Eventually we reached a point where we were able to cross the valley by fording a small brook, and we followed a track into a hillside of coconut-perfumed gorse. It was a trap. The track narrowed as we followed it uphill, until it suddenly ran out. Turning back, we had to reach further inland again before battling our way back to the cliffs.

A little later, I was relieved to see the unmistakable conical top of a round tower, mottled white and grey above the trees in the distance: Ardmore in sight at last! It was tempting for a minute to leg it into the village the short way across the fields, but we headed resolutely on towards Ram's Head to do the job properly. Within minutes the point was in sight, with its elaborate castellated coastguard tower and its spectacular cliffs dropping nearly a hundred feet sheer to the sea below. In the far distance we could now see the cliffscape stretching eastwards, ending in Mine Head, topped by its lighthouse.

At the foot of Ardmore's cliffs there are a number of dramatic caves that can be reached only by boat. One is said to have within it a statue of an underworld monster, another contains a fresh water spring, while a third is called St. Declan's Parlour because of its beauty. Declan was the early Christian founder of the monastic settlement at Ardmore, and his name is attached to

many features of the countryside around, natural and man-made. From the cliff top I looked over in vain to locate another curiosity, a great slab called the Name Rock. For centuries visitors have carved their names on this rock, including the prince who was to become King William IV, who visited Ardmore as a young naval officer towards the end of the eighteenth century.

A daisy-strewn track along the cliff led us down to an elaborately constructed holy well. One could easily be fooled into thinking that it dated back to early Christian times, and I was surprised to discover that the structure around and over the spring was erected shortly after World War I.

In the 1920s a constant visitor from Limerick by the name of O'Rahilly, who had fallen in love with Ardmore, decided for some reason to elevate what was up to then just a simple spring by constructing the monument that can now be seen. He paid for the transport of the stone and a few labourers to help him, but did most of the work himself!

The rough and sometimes invisible track we had been following now became a proper path that led along the cliffs through heather and gorse towards the coastguard signalling station, an elaborate structure with an outside stair. Between this building and the sea we found a modern and much more modest lookout post that dated from the Emergency: a tiny structure not much bigger than the wheelhouse of a small trawler, it must have been a miserable place to stand guard on a winter's night, watching out for an invasion by the Germans or the British.

I was poking about this post trying to imagine the scene back in the forties, when Teresa called me from the cliff edge. There, seventy feet down, lodged on the rocks so securely that it could have been here forever, lay the *Samson* a twin-funnelled construction ship with a crane as high as the ship was long. Against all the efforts of her crew, she had insisted on coming ashore while on her way to Cork one stormy night in the early spring of 1988. The crew were all rescued, and no sooner had the vessel secured herself on the rocks without a soul on board, when a

22

local man absailed down the cliffs onto her deck and 'claimed' the *Samson* as salvage. It must have been a slow period for news, for within hours, newspapermen, photographers, and television people descended on Ardmore. The story was on all the front pages for a few days while the intrepid salvor braved the heavy seas thundering against the vessel's sides, provisions being dropped down to him by friends from the cliffs above. Crowds of sightseers gathered above to see the spectacle of the large ship, which had been treated like a rubber duck by the sea, and the lone salvor awaiting offers.

After some time it became apparent that it was a pointless exercise; the economics of salvaging the *Samson* did not make sense, so the vessel was abandoned for the last time and has rusted here since.

Not far to the east of the watch tower is another castellated structure in ruins, which used to be the local coastguard station. They must have been a hardy bunch of men because they were kept busy in wintertime along this coast in the days of sail. The last of the old sailing ships to succumb near here was the *Teaser*, an eighty-ton lugger which was driven ashore at Ardmore in 1911.

It was on St. Patrick's Day in that year that the worst gales for sixteen years tossed the *Teaser* with her four crew into the bay of Ardmore, where she ran aground on the beach. There she lay on her side, buffeted by breakers, while her crew took to the rigging and hung there praying for rescue. The coastguards and some local people led by the parish priest assembled on the beach to see what they could do; a rocket bearing a line was successfully dropped on to the stricken vessel, but the crew were too exhausted to heave the breeches buoy out. One of the coastguards tried to swim out to the vessel, but had to be rescued by another. Eventually the rescuers managed to haul themselves out into the maelstrom of surf, using the rocket line, and with great difficulty extricated the crew of the *Teaser* from the rigging. Unfortunately all four of the crew died a short time later from exposure and exhaustion.

The parish priest received a gold medal from the Lifeboat Institution for his efforts and two of the coastguards received silver medals and £5 each.

We left the spindly, rusting *Samson*, now becoming a part of the coast here, ignored by the kittiwakes that fly around it. The cliff path was now properly surfaced, and the gentle gradient down towards Ardmore was most welcome. The evening sun was catching flushes of primroses topping out the rich reds and browns of the sculpted sandstone cliffs as we rounded Ram's Head and descended westwards, with the long sandy beaches of Ardmore coming into view ahead.

On the outskirts of Ardmore we came upon our second Holy Well in twenty minutes, and if O'Rahilly's Well is the newest in Ardmore, the well at Teampeall Disert is probably the oldest; indeed from the many carved and incised crosses worn smooth from pilgrims' attentions, it is the most revered. It was here that St. Declan, Bishop of the Decies, is said to have baptised the first Christians in the south of Ireland as early as 402, a full thirty years before St. Patrick came to Ireland.

The ruined church located here, probably predates the other religious buildings in Ardmore, and legend has it that the church was built as a thanksgiving by three Spanish knights who were saved from drowning when their ship foundered in the bay. It consists of two ruined gables and a length of side wall in which there is an unusual doorway where the keystone of the arch is upside-down! The Goban Saor, a mythical Celtic mastermason who is reputed to have built most of the ancient buildings in Ardmore, could hardly be responsible for this. In fact, close examination reveals that it is a clever mason's trick, and the keystone reverts to a more normal configuration a couple of inches back from the face.

The Cliff Hotel, our destination in Ardmore, clings to the cliff side, providing its principal rooms with fine views over the bay; indeed I do not know of another dining room in the country that can boast such a panorama. Great white gannets put on day-long performances for the Cliff Hotel residents, diving spectacularly into the sea, bobbing up again like corks after a few seconds, and making a long splashing takeoff, fish in beak, before climbing to forty feet or more and starting again. Guillemots and cormorants fish from the water's surface, and while their dives may not be as showy as the gannets, they stay submerged a long time and travel sometimes a considerable distance from their starting point. Ordinary gulls and great blackbacks cruise up and down the rocky water's edge, watching for their chances on land or sea. Across the narrow, neatly kept terraced garden between the hotel and the sea, the terrestrial birds parade: wood pigeons, rock pigeons and crows pass to and fro, while sparrows, blackbirds and robins forage in the hedges and on the lawns.

The historical centre of attraction of Ardmore is the round tower, the classic silhouette of which, standing nearly one hundred feet tall, is visible for miles around. Legend has it that St. Declan built this tower in three nights, leaving off each night at one of the offsets or string courses, which are not to be found in any other round tower in Ireland. He would have gone on building it up to the very clouds, but for an old woman who watched him every day, and was constantly asking, 'Wisha Declan, how high are you going to build it at all?' She so annoyed Declan that he finished it in a point and gave up.

In reality the tower was built long after Declan's day, probably in the twelfth century, when the monastic city was at the peak of its importance. It was one of the latest and most architecturally refined *cloigteach* or belfries to be built, and the bell that hung in the top of the tower could apparently be heard in Glenmore, eight miles away. Each of the stone blocks used in its construction was cut to the required curve; I like to think that the idea may have arisen to use naturally curved stone like that to be seen at the east end of Whiting Bay, but eventually it was all quarried at Slievegrine, a few miles inland. Tradition has it that the stone was brought to Ardmore 'without horse or wheel' and the tower built 'without sound of hammer'. As late as the last century, some of the rejected stones still lay about the quarry. The original stone cross at the top of the tower was shot off in the early eighteenth century by a man shooting at 'red-legged daws' or choughs, which were much more common at that time and may have even nested in the tower. It was replaced in the last century when the conical roof underwent repairs.

An unusual feature of the inside of the tower is the projecting stones that have been carved to represent animal heads; it has been suggested that these were done as a pastime by the men building the tower.

Many of the round towers around the country were surrounded by Norse invaders, but the round tower in Ardmore holds the unusual distinction of being the only tower that was besieged by attackers bearing firearms. It happened in the late summer of 1642, when Irish forces held Ardmore Castle, which lay to the east of the church. Their presence in Ardmore meant they were in a position to seize the substantial harvest from the lands to the east, essential to the continuance of the Irish army as a fighting force. The castle was manned by over a hundred men, and an additional forty men occupied the round tower; although the Irish had sufficient supplies to withstand a long siege, the defenders of the tower had only two muskets between them.

The English approached on 26 August with a force of 60 cavalry and 400 infantry armed with muskets, and quickly surrounded the Irish, occupying some of the outhouses of the castle and the church itself, but were unable to gain further ground due to the hail of musket fire that rained down on them from the castle and the tower. They were content to wait, however, because a piece of artillery capable of reducing the castle and the tower, a culverin, was on its way by sea.

The culverin arrived the following morning, and for three hours the English dragged it up from the beach and manhandled it into place within 'half a Musket shot of the castle', as a contemporary account described. The Irish watched with increasing trepidation, pouring a hail of musket fire on the artillerymen, but the English protected themselves successfully with 'wooll packes' and not one casualty was suffered.

As soon as the Irish saw that the dreaded culverin was ready to fire, they flew the white flag: in order to save the lives of the women and children, an unconditional surrender was offered. The English were delighted with themselves, having captured the stronghold in a little more than twenty-four hours with no casualties, but that did not soften their treatment of the prisoners. As soon as the women and children were let go with their clothing and belongings, the men, all 117 of them, were immediately hanged.

The present ruins and graveyard occupy only about a sixth of the monastic settlement. During the last century the foundations of the tower were opened up for examination and were found to have been excavated through already existing graves, indicating that the graveyard has been continually in use for a thousand years at least.

East of the cathedral is a small structure in which St. Declan is said to have been buried; it also has been called 'Leaba Deglan' or 'Declan's Bed'. It has many of the characteristics of an early oratory, although it was restored and re-roofed in 1726, a restoration that may have destroyed all but a few of its original features. On the saints' feast days, during the eighteenth and nineteenth centuries and probably earlier, local people would sell small portions of what they maintained were St. Declan's ashes to pilgrims, in spite of a tradition that said that Declan's ashes were not to be disturbed 'while water ran, while grasses grew'. The locals cheerfully disregarded this admonishment, and over the centuries many tons of these sacred ashes were miraculously dispensed in this manner, the clay floor of the oratory having dropped to its present level by the early decades of the last century.

In medieval times, the saint's skull would be put on display for veneration during the pattern. Once, when being taken down, it fell, knocking a hole in the forehead. It was carefully wrapped, and taken to a silversmith in Youghal to have the hole repaired with a silver plate. While working on the fragile skull, the silversmith dropped it and this time it smashed into tiny fragments. Faced with the wrath of the people who made good livings from the pattern, the silversmith quietly at night retrieved the skull of an executed murderer from the spikes of the Clock Gate and, fitting it with a silver plate, sent it back to Ardmore, where it was revered for many years!

The ruined cathedral of Ardmore is unique for the Irish Romanesque arcade carvings on the west gable, depicting biblical scenes. It was built and added to at various periods from the sixth to the twelfth century, and in the nave there is a rich collection of gravestones spanning the entire period up to the nineteenth century.

Ardmore Castle has now disappeared without trace, but there must be very few old houses in the village that do not contain some stones from it. It must have been a substantial castle when it was built in the thirteenth century; Perkin Warbeck, the pretender to the English throne, 'slept here' in 1492 with his army camped in the fields around, before marching eastwards to besiege Waterford, and Sir Walter Raleigh leased it, together with the 'manor' of Ardmore, in 1591. Its last inhabitant appears to have been Sir Edward Harris, Chief Justice of the Court of Common Pleas, who was lord and master of all he surveyed in the early seventeenth century. He collected feudal taxes of one-tenth of all that was produced in his manor, until the courtyard of the castle was often 'crowded with flocks, herds, and gorged with corn'. Harris had a family of thirteen children and so many servants that when he went visiting, he rode at the head of a column that was more than a mile long!

Ardmore today is a sleepy, picturesque village during autumn, winter and spring, but comes alive in summer, when the small population is more than doubled by holidaymakers, most of whom stay in a city of caravans behind the beach. The remoteness of the village has made it a popular place for writers and artists, and it is proud to count Molly Keane, Norah McGuinness, Claud Cockburn and Joan Jameson amongst those who have found solace and inspiration there.

I was very pleased to have completed the first step in my trek to the Suir so easily; but for a few slight obstacles, I found the coastline could be followed closely. The constant variety of topography and ever-changing surroundings and views, even in the short stretch we had covered, had made it a marvellous walk, and had whetted my appetite for what was to come.

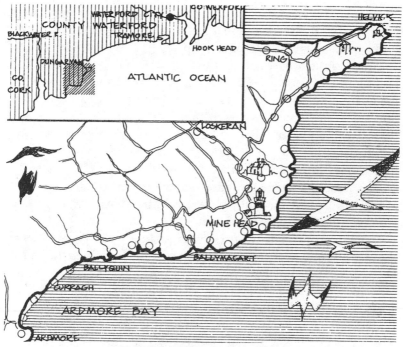

ARDMORE TO RING

The stretch of coast between Ardmore and Ring seemed a bit long for one day's comfortable walk, so I planned an overnight halt about halfway, at Mine Head. The *Bord Failte Guide to Guesthouses*, however, had no listing for this remote part of the coast, so I was left in a quandary as to where I could stay, if indeed there was any accommodation available. Thumbing through the telephone directory some weeks before setting out, I found a number for Mine Head Lighthouse. On an impulse I picked up the phone and rang to enquire if the lighthouse keeper would know of anyone in the area who might put me up. The puzzled man at first thought I wanted to stay with him, and protested that it would be out of the question, but when he understood what I wanted he told me the local postmistress might be able to help.

Cathleen Tobin is the postmistress at Loskeran, a couple of

miles inland from Mine Head, and although there turned out to be no bed and breakfast houses in the area, she kindly arranged for her sister next door to put me up.

So the stretch between Ardmore and Ring was thus split into two handy sections, about nine or ten miles to Loskeran, and a further five or six to Ring. However, there was one detail I had omitted to take into account. Although it was clear that much of this coastline was nearly three hundred feet above sea level, my one-inch maps did not emphasise that every time a stream ran into the sea this three hundred feet would have to be descended and ascended. It turned out that there were seven streams entering the sea between Ardmore Bay and Mine Head, adding about 4,000 vertical feet to the journey!

We set out from the Cliff Hotel in Ardmore on a May morning that was humid and sunny. Overnight a thick sea mist had blanketed the coast, but by dawn it had partially retreated, leaving glistening jewels of dew on the early summer vegetation. Mine Head, normally clearly visible from Ram's Head, was still hidden under a hazy curtain. The greeny-blue waters of Ardmore Bay were calm and clear, and the seabed and submerged rocks could be seen in sharp detail extending out from the foot of the cliffs.

Down by the beach, a lady pointed out St. Declan's Rock, a barnacled, seaweed-covered boulder perched on the shore near the sea wall. There is an opening in the wall with steps leading down for pilgrims who wish to pay a visit to this venerable rock. Wondrous cures have been ascribed for those prepared to circumnavigate the rock on their knees, praying all the while, followed by snaking under it (no mean task) three times. The people of west Waterford must be amongst the world's finest tall-story tellers, because the legend of how this rock came to be where it is takes some beating. It is 'handed down' that when St. Declan was ordained a bishop and left Rome to travel back to Ireland, he left behind him by mistake the bells he had cast there for his new cathedral in Ardmore. On his arrival in Ardmore, however, after a couple of months travelling across Europe, and to the delight of the locals, the bells and a set of rich vestments sailed into the bay on the back of this boulder!

There may have been some pagan significance in this stone,

and as was common in other places, it may have been de-paganised by being used as a mass altar. Having read many stories about this phenomenon, I was most disappointed at the reality; how this insignificant flotsam-and-fishing-line-festooned rock could have inspired such reverence and legend is beyond understanding.

The sand of Ardmore beach, like that of Youghal, covers a bed of peat which is exposed from time to time by storm action. In 1879 a *crannog*, or ancient lake dwelling, was discovered in the sand of the beach by the Waterford naturalist, R.J. Ussher. The remains were so well preserved that the internal partition walls of wattle were still in position, showing how the rooms had been laid out. The dwelling was probably built when the sea level was much lower, on a lagoon which existed where the strand is now, separated from the sea by a sand spit, and a narrow easily defensible causeway would have connected the *crannog* with the shore. I was told that the remains are visible at low tide, but we saw no trace of it as we passed by.

As we walked along the beach, a mahogony-faced farm worker in green wellington boots and a tweed jacket passed us riding a great battered black bicycle, a machine known in that part of the country as a High Nellie. It was as if the road which ran past here, connecting Ardmore to the village of Curragh until it was inundated in the last century, still existed, if only in spirit. The loss of the road made things very difficult in the summer for the local people, because the beach was owned by the Odell family, the local landlords, and access was forbidden when the family was picnicking there. This meant that the locals had to make a wide detour inland by the remaining road, a situation which lasted until the Odells departed from Ardmore, handing over ownership of the beach and cliffs to the people.

A heron stood motionless at the low-water mark near the remains of a wrecked ship, the keel, ribs and propeller shaft coated in seaweed and barnacles. Nearby, a jumbled and exotic-looking piece of natural limestone protruded from the beach, a part of the extensive bedrock that gives this coastline its form and colour.

Between Ardmore beach and Curragh beach a flat limestone peninsula extends into the sea, carrying sandy-soiled fields down to the high water mark. As we crossed over this, our feet quickly became soaked, our boots absorbing from the grass the thick dew of the previous night. Soon we were squelching along with water squirting out through the lace holes, disturbing a brisk massacre by blackbirds and rooks of the myriad slugs feeding on a failed crop of carrots, similar to what we had seen at Whiting Bay.

The coastal rocks between Ardmore beach and Curragh presented a spectacular scene with the tide out; rows upon rows of ragged spikes, a natural *chevaux-de-frise* turned on the sea. They were light grey in colour at the top of the beach, toning down darker and darker as they extended seawards, eventually taking on a dark brown mantle of seaweed.

Scattered across the rocky peninsula, the bent figures of periwinkle pickers foraged among the fissures, their voices distant as they called to one another, making a duet with the constant lark song.

An elderly fisherman in a navy jumper and very baggy grey canvas trousers, rolled to his knees, stood in the gentle wavelets of the dropping tide, unwinding a long net; the misty surroundings gave the scene a dreamlike quality, like a soft-focus passage from a surrealist movie.

Three great sheets of limestone interrupt the stretches of sandy beach in Ardmore Bay, punctuating our walk with rich beds of seaweed, colourful stones and rockpools. Just before Ballyquin beach, the limestone changed character from fiercely rugged to great rounded humped shapes like a fossilised herd of elephants, which made for some strenuous knee-bending exercises as we scrambled over them. At Ballyquin the remains of a lime kiln with a wide stone arch stood sentinel over the beach, the road to it washed away by eroding tides. Beyond the kiln the bedrock changed again, here metamorphosed by great heat and pressure splitting and twisting it, and filling the fissures that rive it with white feldspar.

We were not far from the end of the beach when, in a matter of minutes, the mist that had been covering the cliffs dissipated, and for the first time that day we could see in detail what lay in store for us. I was glad to see what appeared to be a path, starting at a ruined summerhouse and wending its way up along the cliffs, which were not sheer, but shelved into the sea.

Inland from the end of the beach, a fine Georgian house with a yellow-painted facade stood overlooking the bay against a densely wooded background. Between the house and the beach a daisy-speckled meadow, almost a lawn, had all the signs of having fought a losing battle with the sea. Generations of waves had undermined the meadow, which dropped in a series of grassy terraces to the sand.

As we reached the end of the beach, we came upon more winkle-pickers, a man and a woman moving slowly among the rocks, bent double. Sharing their stand, and taking as little notice of them as they were taking of it, stood a heron, which reluctantly moved off as I approached.

'Would you know anything about the ruined summerhouse on the cliff?' I asked the nearest winkle-picker, a woman in her thirties.

'Well, it was owned by the Fuges originally, but I don't know what it was called,' she said, straightening up and shading her eyes with her hand.

'The Fuges were the landlords of all the lands around, you know. The nuns had it then, years and years ago as a kind of holiday place for the sisters, but I don't ever remember it being lived in.'

I remembered that the nave of Ardmore Cathedral had many slabs commemorating members of the Fuges family, spanning the years between 1711 and 1976.

She told me that the periwinkles were very scarce.

'It must be pollution or something; they should be very good now, shouldn't they?' she asked as she dug her hand into the red plastic bucket she carried and let a handful of the shellfish run through her fingers.

'The children love eating them. Oh jay they're horrible, they takes them out with a pin. I wouldn't touch them myself,' she said, shuddering at the thought, a strange reply when she had just filled a bucket with the things.

'The white ones are no good I suppose,' I said pointing to another variety of mollusc on the rocks that seemed to be more numerous than the periwinkle.

'I don't think so, not completely.'

'Well I hope the children enjoy them anyway,' I said as I left her, seeing Teresa had gone a long way ahead.

'Oh, they will, they'll spend hours in the garden picking them with a pin,' she replied, as she bent again to her task.

A little more than an hour after leaving the Cliff Hotel, we reached the eastern extremity of the beach, where a woodland stream emerges from the trees and forms a deep pool against a shingle bank before it reluctantly runs down to the sea. The woods clothe a picturesque valley going inland, its floor covered with wild flowers. We paused a few minutes to watch young trout leaping out of the water of the pool and plopping back, attracted by the abundance of flies hovering over the surface.

Our feet had had a chance to dry out while crossing the beaches, but as we started ascending the cliffs through long grass, we were saturated again, this time up to our knees. By the time we had reached the 200 feet contour, the sun had burnt off the earlier mist and the temperature was climbing.

After our walk along the beaches, the cliffs were a real contrast, and difficult and all as it was to beat our way through the early summer's growth of gorse and brambles, the narcotic effect of the sweet perfumes of shrubs and herbs mixed in a sea breeze gave them a magic of their own. A few hundred yards along the grassy track following the cliffs, we came to a carefully engineered and well-constructed terraced track. Although very overgrown, it made for pleasant walking for a while until it vanished into a sea of gorse, and we diverted into a wheat field.

At the western end of Crobally Lower, a deep chasm, the first of many we were to come across along this stretch of coast, penetrated nearly a mile inland, at the bottom of which a tiny stream trickled its way to the sea. Having taken the high cliff-path, we had now to give up those sweltering few hundred feet we had earlier gained to drop down the steep sides of the ravine, and struggle up the other side. The sight of two shelducks taking off from the shingle beach offered only slight consolation!

On the cliff edge again, the path wended its way around some dramatically beautiful inlets, sometimes disappearing over the precipice where the sea had eroded away great chunks of the shore, certainly not a place for vertigo sufferers. The views at that stage were all behind us to the west where we could see Blackball Head again, rising above the low-lying ground inland from Ardmore. It was a phenomenon I thoroughly enjoyed at every stage of this walk; looking back at places I had passed through and had got to know, places that months before were only bland names and locations on a map examined minutely during a Dublin winter, places that had now taken on colour and character. With just a turn of my head, I could look ahead at the yet unknown coast slowly taking shape ahead, the pleasure of discovering it before me.

The air temperature was still rising as we descended another ravine, clambering gingerly down its steep sides through extensive bunches of primroses. A family of choughs rose as we crossed the stream at the bottom, at the far side of which we ran into a jungle of gorse and thorn bushes. There were tracks through the bushes, made by cattle, but those we followed narrowed and eventually petered out. For the first time since Youghal bridge, we had to retrace our steps and seek an alternative way. At the stream we turned inland, and within a few minutes had found a track that brought us back up to the cliffs again.

Not far on, another gorge, this one also thick with thorn bushes, blocked our way. Instead of dropping down and joining battle with the undergrowth, we decided this time to follow the contours around the inlet and, we hoped, back out onto the cliffs. So inland we went, crossing a newly ploughed field which eerily produced a thick ground mist all of its own, which rolled along the turned earth only to disappear as it reached the adjoining meadow. It was a most unusual sight, and we noticed as we walked through it that it had a very unpleasant smell.

After about half-a-mile of trying unsuccessfully to find a way across the ravine, we reached a public road. I was unsure of exactly where we were at this stage, having lost track of our progress along the cliffs, so to be sure that we would not go too far out of our way, we turned right and east. Less than a mile further on we reached a junction, the right turn of which I assumed would take us down into Ballymacart Cove. On the corner, a row of saggy-roofed farm buildings surrounded a haggard, on the gate of which hung a row of grey longjohns.

Following the road downhill, it was not long before we could see the inlet of Ballymacart Cove ahead of us and about 300 feet below. The road to the cove was carefully designed to ensure an even gradient, which meant it was regularly hairpinned, doubling back on itself as it lost altitude, like a trans-Pyrenean highway. Our feet were by now feeling the journey, because the constant wetting and drying had washed out the oil in the skin of our soles, making them more tender. Having miserable feet meant that joys such as cascades of bluebells and sprays of primroses had little effect on our spirits. A glance at the map showed that we were at best only halfway to Mine Head, and our feet would get a lot worse before they got better.

Ballymacart has a little beach, its sand pierced by craggy rocks with tiaras of seapinks; it is a mystery how such plants could survive here at all. We sat down on the sand beside one of these rocks to eat our lunch of spiced-beef sandwiches and tea. The spiced beef was a mistake, we both agreed later: it served only to further feed our thirst.

After lunch and a quick massage of our sore feet, we set off again, passing the ruins of a substantial stone building which, whatever it used to be, must have been the reason for the well-built and expensive road into this little cove. A disused and overgrown roadway climbs up the eastern side of Ballymacart Cove, interrupted by frequent subsidence, and we followed this uphill to the cliffs again.

We passed a couple of *gallans* on our way through the fields to the next deep ravine, which this time had no thorn bushes or gorse choking it, but had extremely steep sides. I did not like the idea of taking another long diversion inland; at this rate of going, there was no guessing what the ultimate mileage to Mine Head would be, and whether we would get there before dark. I did a little investigation, scrambling down part of the way, and decided to give it a try. I called up to Teresa to follow me carefully, ignoring the fact that if one of us fell it would be a major problem. I was scared stiff, although I did not let Teresa know, and she assumed I knew what I was doing! We followed, partially on foot and partially on our bottoms, what could have only been a rabbit track, and, to my great relief, eventually made it safely down to the little stream gurgling along the bottom of the valley. Following the stream to the shore, we found a tiny picturesque beach, the cliffs at the back of which were made up of crushed and twisted metamorphic rock riddled like tipsy cake with streaks of white feldspar, and overhung with thick clumps of yellow vetch.

As we climbed up to the cliffs again, I saw that Ram's Head

was still visible in the distance behind us, seeming to mock our progress; I wondered would we ever lose sight of it. But relief was at hand! We had just passed into a townland called on the map Ballynaharda or 'the high place' and, although it is not actually higher than the surrounding land, by some quirk of topography it seems to overlook all around it. For the first time since leaving the beach at Ardmore, we could again see for some distance in front of us, and we gave a spirited whoop of relief and delight when the black-and-white lines of Mine Head Lighthouse, something we had been watching for all day, came into sight on the cliffs ahead. At the same time Ram's Head finally disappeared behind, and we had a new coastline to look forward to, stretching away to the east, green finger after green finger of cliff reaching into a sea whose blue colour grew deeper as the afternoon wore on.

We had yet another inpenetrable ravine to deal with before reaching the lighthouse, but the fact that we were within sight of our goal, and this would be the last to be negotiated, gave us a new lease of life. We headed inland to cross the ravine at Hacketstown bridge, passing on our way the ruins of two fine houses with elaborate chimney stacks and brick string courses. They stood in the middle of a field, with no road and no sign of any gardens or earthworks around them, as if they had just dropped out of the sky. They had a spooky air about them, and as we passed the second one we started as a huge rust-brown hare with grey-tipped ears darted out of it across our path and into a clump of gorse. We learned later that the occupants of the houses had been burnt out as a result of a land dispute not many years before. The gardens and the avenue must have been ploughed shortly after the event, because there is no trace of them now.

We reached the public road and followed it around and back out to the cliffs and Mine Head. The lighthouse and the keeper's house were surrounded by a high whitewashed stone wall and there were signs discouraging trespassers, so we went around the outside and sat on the cliff edge just under the tower. Mine Head Lighthouse came into operation in 1851 to mark the entrance to Dungarvan Harbour, and to act as an intermediate point between Hook Lighthouse in County Wexford and Ballycotton in County

Cork. The architect was George Halpin, who must have had problems administering the contract, because, before the building was finished, the contractor upped and left in a hurry to California where the great Gold Rush was in progress, causing a delay of twelve months in its completion.

Teresa and I were on a high, having had a fairly rough day during which the ravines, wet grass and inability to see any distance ahead had taken their toll on our morale. Although our walking for the day was not finished, to sit there on the tip of Mine Head, surrounded by thrift and yellow vetch, under a sun which had now a friendly warmth in place of the earlier heat, made us feel marvellous!

At Mine Head the cliffs are spectacular, not sheer, but shelving down into the sea at an angle of 50 degrees. The lighthouse, with its great light permanently revolving, stands out on the very edge of the 200-foot high head; to pass it, one has to go inland around it. That day it was a chocolate box scene: the sky, the sea, and the wildflower-covered cliff edge providing a perfect frame to the black and white striped lighthouse.

The coastal cliffs beyond Dungarvan Harbour stretched grey-blue far into the haze in the east, against a deep blue sea that was patterned with drifts and currents. To the west the coast receded in shadowed backdrops to Ram's Head, beyond which Cable Island could be seen off the coast of County Cork. This balmy Mine Head was so opposite to what I had expected: all I had read about the place had led me to picture it in the throes of the cold, dark winds and rains of winter.

Many a proud ship came to grief on or near these cliffs in such conditions. One of the last of the windjammers to be seen in the area ended its last voyage here. The *Marechal de Noailles*, a small clipper of 2,707 tons, had set out from a French port in the winter of 1912 with a cargo for New Caledonia in the South Pacific. Caught in strong gales off the coast of Cork, she had attempted to run before the storm, but was forced aground at the foot of Mine Head, with every great wave hammering her nearer to destruction. The crew of twenty-four held on precariously, awaiting rescue, while the lighthouse keeper sent word to nearby Helvic Harbour for the lifeboat and the coastguards.

The Helvic lifeboat was launched and fought its way around the coast to where the French ship lay, but it was impossible to get alongside without being dashed on the rocks. Meanwhile, the coastguards, including Messrs Barry and Neal, the silver medal heroes of the *Teaser* shipwreck the year before, arrived from Ardmore with their rocket equipment on a trailer, and began to set it up on the clifftop. They were joined by Father O'Shea, the intrepid rescuer-cum parish priest, and some of the townsfolk.

Before long the breeches buoy rocket was fired, taking a line to the French ship. The French, however, unfamiliar with the workings of the buoy, make the line fast, instead of hauling it in and bringing on board the heavier line carrying the breeches. Instructions hailed over the howling wind were not understood by the French, who spoke no English, so for a period the rescue operation ground to a halt. During this confusion a strong wave swept one of the French sailors overboard, but he made it to the rocks. Coastguard Neal climbed down through the squalling rain in the gloom and succeeded in bringing the Frenchman to safety. This proved to be the saving stroke for all the crew, because it was now possible to explain to the sailor (through the lighthouse-keeper's wife, who had some French) the workings of the breeches buoy, and he was able to pass this on to his shipmates by loud-hailer.

Another rocket was fired; this time the gear was fully deployed, and the crew were all taken off safely. The last to leave the vessel was the captain, with the shop's dog clutched tightly in his lap!

It was not always the forces of nature that caused shipwrecks off this coast. Between February 1917 and September 1918, seventeen ships were torpedoed or otherwise sunk by German U-boats in the vicinity of Mine Head, with the loss of over one hundred lives. During World War II many of the casualties of convoy actions out to sea were washed up along this coast. One of the most poignant occurrences happened in the last few months of the war, when a Polish sailor, having survived weeks in an open boat while his companions died one by one, made it to shore just under the cliffs nearby. In spite of suffering from frostbite and exposure, he managed to crawl to the fields above before collapsing. He was found by a passing farmer, who carried the sailor to his home and put him in front of a roaring fire to warm him up. This was apparently the wrong thing to do with a frostbite victim, and led to the unfortunate man having to have both his legs amputated.

From my map it seemed that we still had a couple of miles at least to go before we reached our destination for the night — the five crossroads at Loskeran. So we reluctantly picked ourselves up out of the mattress-like grass of the headland and made our way inland.

By this stage, the combination of the warm sun and the spiced-beef lunch had made us very thirsty, and when we met a couple of farmers outside a house we asked if we could have a drink of water. The older man kindly got a cup from the house and filled it from a tap in the yard. I never tasted water so good! He watched us with obvious satisfaction and pride as we drank, and told us that the water should be cool, because it came from 65 feet down. When we told him where we were heading and where we had come from, he gestured to his companion, saying he was just going up to Loskeran and would give us a lift in his car. It took us milliseconds to shrug off any principles about this being a walking trip, and we gladly accepted. We climbed into the younger man's battered car and made space for ourselves among the bailing twine and plastic bags. Within minutes the last mile of our day's journey was eaten up and we were being greeted by Cathleen Tobin at Loskeran Post Office. She was a good-humoured young woman full of interest in our walk, and one of the few people I came across during my journey who saw nothing strange about wanting to walk the coast. We sat for a while in the sun outside the post office chatting to her and telling her where we had been, and then she brought us next door to meet our hostess for the night, her sister, Marion Gough.

The Gough house was a neatly kept bungalow surrounded by manicured gardens with a rich variety of flowering plants and shrubs. While we ate our evening meal, I was delighted to see rabbits running and scampering about in the field next door. What might be a 'pretty' sight for city people, however, was, from the look of the elaborate fence around the garden, a serious problem in the country. Marion told us that when the rabbits are not decimating the vegetables, the calves from the field next door were consuming the griselinia hedge, which apparently they consider a delicacy.

After dinner we wandered a half mile down the road to the 'local', known as John Paul's. Set in a grove of conifers beside a crossroads with rusty petrol pumps standing sentinel outside, what must have been one of the most unspoilt pubs in Ireland was undergoing modernisation.

We entered through a porch stacked high with packages and bundles of newspapers, and found ourselves in what appeared to be a cottage kitchen. We almost backed out, embarrassed, thinking we had entered a private house, but then noticed a small group of men and women sitting in the gloom around a fire with drinks in their hands. One of the women sporadically entertained the rest with a Neil Diamond song, breaking off frequently and exclaiming 'God, what great lyrics. I only wish my voice was up to them!'

There was no counter in the room, but through a doorway we could hear the clink of bottles; following the sound, we found ourselves in a long narrow room with a bar along one side. Behind the bar was a thin white-haired man, whom afterwards we learned was John Paul himself.

The building had been extended, and the place was in the process of being fitted out with new seating and elaborate veneered panelling; only the ancient timber-sheeted ceiling, glistening with a thick brown coat of nicotine, remained of what had been before. We ordered a drink, and while he served us, John Paul probed gently, in a roundabout way, for the answers to the three questions country people are usually too polite to ask directly of strangers — 'What's your name?/ Where do you come from?/ and What are you doing here?' He used a little Gaelic phrase here and there in his conversation and, saying he was fond of the language, sought for a hint of what 'kind' of Irish people we were by asking us did we speak it.

Before long we were joined by Micheal Tobin, Cathleen's husband, who introduced us to John Paul, and mentioned that I was interested in the history and folklore of the area. It seemed as if I had come to the right place, because between John Paul himself, Micheal and some other locals who came in, we were regaled for the next two hours with stories of shipwrecks, the 'Troubles' and local intrigues. There were many reminiscences in particular about John Paul's late father, Willie, a legendary figure in the area. Once a rather posh visitor asked Willie where the toilets were, and was told, 'You see that door over there? Well go through that, and your toilet is all the way to the Comeraghs!'

Micheal Tobin gave us a lift back to the five crossroads at the end of an informative and amusing evening, and insisted that we come into his house for a cup of tea before bed. We enjoyed an hour of his and Cathleen's company before we finally said goodnight and headed next door to bed.

The following morning we set off early for Helvick and Ring, looking forward to a change in topography as the cliffs dropped down to sea level around Dungarvan harbour. After the warm sunshine of the previous evening, a thick mist now lay over the countryside, but we headed south for the sea, all businesslike at the start of our day, in spite of the twenty-yard visibility.

Passing an old cottage whose walls were decorated with thousands of bottle caps which must have taken a lifetime of drinking to collect, we came to a gate across the boreen we were following. On a tree beside the gate was a sign with the legend 'Preserved, fur and feather. Persons enter these lands at their own risk. Signed C. Walshe'. It was hard to know whether this was actually a threat, or a warning by a farmer who had been stung by someone who had abused the privilege of being able freely to cross farmland. It did not augur well anyway, and we decided to avoid the boreen and go over the fields to the sea. Crossing fence after countless fence and avoiding cattle, it was nearly an hour before I spotted the ravine we were making for, on the western side of which was a *cromlech* I wanted to see. Unfortunately the diversion we had taken had led us to the eastern side of the ravine, and a jungle of thorn trees stood between us and the other side, so I reluctantly decided to give the *cromlech* a miss and carry on eastwards.

We made our way down through thick bracken, following a cattle track into a magical valley, the mist lending an unreal quality to the surroundings, fading out the tops of the Scots pines and seeming to muffle the sound of the rushing stream below.

Unlike the other streams we had crossed the previous day, this one was a real 'River of No Return', a raging torrent of the kind I am more used to seeing in mountain terrain. As we walked beside it, looking for a suitable crossing place, a dipper emerged from the turbulent waters in the shallows to perch, dipping and dripping, on a rock. It was streams like this one that supplied the essential water needs of the many iron-smelting works that existed in this area four hundred years ago. Sir Walter Raleigh was granted the lands of Mine Head as part of the thousands of acres he received in west Waterford in return for his service in the Irish wars. It did not take long for the entrepreneur in Raleigh, who was responsible for the introduction of potatoes and tobacco into Europe, to recognise the mineral potential in his new lands, and by 1595 he had identified many locations where iron ore could be mined economically. Fifty Cornish miners were imported to work the mines, and smelting mills were established, fuelled by the plentiful forestry in the Blackwater valley.

By 1604 Raleigh had fallen from favour and had been forced to dispose of his estates for a pittance to the Earl of Cork, who expanded the works considerably, and developed the port of Youghal to ship out the iron and steel. The workings at Mine Head were particularly noted for the suitability of their fine steel for sword-making, which was probably their downfall, for they were destroyed during the 1641 Rebellion.

The last hundred yards before the stream entered the sea, it cascades down a series of waterfalls, maintaining its 'mountainy' image to the last. Eventually finding a series of slippery stepping stones, we crossed the torrent gingerly, and ascended the slope on the far side, towards the sea cliffs.

Here the mist became thicker, and we were unable to see not only the terrain ahead, but for most of the time even the actual cliff edge. All sounds were muffled by the moisture-laden air, including the sea crashing on the rocks far below, leaving only the swishing of the wet grass as we walked through it and the twittering of invisible swallows over our heads. The path along the cliffs was lined with bluebells, each flower almost doubled over with its burden of moisture.

Two hours after departing from Loskeran, I decided there was little point, and probably some danger, in wading blind through a very wet fog on a cliff edge, and we would be better following the public road for a while until the fog had lifted. My map suggested that we could connect with a road close by, at the hamlet of Ballycurreen South, running parallel to the coast, so we headed north across the fields to find it.

Within a few minutes we reached the road at a gathering of small cottages grouped around a large prosperous-looking farmhouse with Dutch gables, a contemporary version of the medieval *clachan* or farm village. As we followed the tarmac towards Helvick, the mist thinned a little, and I saw that only a narrow field separated us from the sea. A short while later the mist lifted completely, dramatically unveiling the prominent and bulbous point of Helvick Head. The road turned away from the sea at this point, so we made our way towards the promontory across the fields, climbing to the head's highest point, 263 feet above sea level. This must be a great viewpoint, but there was still a lot of mist about to the north and east which denied us a first sight of Dungarvan harbour and the cliffs to the east.

Avoiding a herd of cattle surrounding a large muscular bull, we escaped down a boreen just behind a summerhouse, built in the last century by the west Waterford landowners, the Villiers Stewarts. As we left the boreen, the pier at Helvick came into view, overlooked by a well-maintained row of coastguards' cottages. We followed the road past the pier and out to a little cove under the Villiers Stewart house, to have our lunch.

The weather was beginning to warm up, and just as well, because we had got soaked walking through wet fields, and were beginning to feel a little chilly. We sat on a worn-out seat and tucked into a lunch of tinned corned beef, apples and coffee, which with the improvement in the weather raised our soggy spirits. Thus rested and provisioned, we set out again, turning west for the first time since Kinsalebeg, and heading for Ring, about a mile and a half away.

Standing above the harbour in Helvick is an imposing monument erected in 1957 and unveiled by Kathleen Clarke, wife of Thomas Clarke, one of the executed leaders of the 1916 Rising. The stone-carved legend, 'Erin's Hope', is followed by a poetic description of the abortive 'invasion' carried out by the Fenians here in 1867. The story of this latter-day D-Day reads like the script of a hilarious farce.

After the American Civil War, the Irish-American Fenians were able with little difficulty to get their hands on large numbers of war surplus guns for the forthcoming Irish rebellion. The Fenian movement in the United States was a very open organisation, and since the English had supported the southern states during the Civil War, the US government for a while at least was prepared to turn a blind eye to its activities. These Fenians abroad were split on the question of how to obtain freedom for Ireland, one faction wanting to supply and support a rebellion in the old country, the other to annoy the English directly and disrupt their relations with the US, by carrying out raids over the border into Canada.

In 1867 the Irish Fenians, tired of waiting for their transatlantic allies to make up their minds, rose in rebellion against the Crown. It was a disastrous and ignominious failure and, although there was little bloodshed, hundreds of Fenians ended up in prison. A month after the rising, a brigantine left New York with a squad of American Fenians and thousands of guns for the Irish. When it arrived off the Sligo coast, prearranged signals were made without success, so the captain went ashore to see if he could make contact with the local Fenians.

While he had gone, there was an argument on board which

resulted in two of the crew being shot. Meanwhile, the local pilot, thinking the vessel could use his services, arrived on board. He was told the boat was bound for Glasgow from Spain with a cargo of fruit, and when he clearly did not believe this, he was seized and put in the brig. The captain returned, having found out that the rebellion had failed, and only in County Cork would he find enough remaining Fenians to make use of the guns. They set sail immediately, taking with them the hapless pilot.

Strong gales prevented them from landing on the coast of Cork, and they were blown eastwards until they lay off Helvick Head. A local fishing hooker was hailed, and the fishermen agreed to take two men ashore; when they pulled alongside, thirty-two Fenians jumped over the brigantine's side and onto the fishing boat! Somewhat overloaded, it was quickly run into the shore at Ballinagoul.

During the course of these events, the local coastguards had been watching with great interest, and were probably aware that the Navy had been searching the west coast for a suspicious vessel during the past fortnight. Seeing the number of men landing, they decided the prudent thing to do was to pass the buck, and they notified the Royal Irish Constabulary in Dungarvan.

The Fenians, who must have looked a bit out-of-place in their foreign clothing, split up on landing and set out by different routes for Cork. The RIC, however, had thrown out a cordon, and by nightfall had rounded up most of the invaders. The brigantine, after standing by offshore for a few days awaiting a favourable signal, was sailed back to America without a single weapon being unloaded!

Most of the captured Fenians were persuaded to apologise to the authorities and were deported back to America. The remaining hardnosed rebels who refused to apologise must have been regarded as harmless, because not one of them remained in jail for more than two years! At the trial the fishermen who had brought the Fenians ashore proved uncooperative, pleading deafness and loss of memory, and one of them identifying the judge as one of the Americans!

Teresa and I wandered along the meandering road towards Ring, taking a brief detour down to the pier at Ballinagoul. The

Scottish engineer, Alexander Nimmo, designed the pier, and also planned a model village nearby. However, his village plans were not carried out and, instead, the place developed organically in a maze of little boreens and potato fields, where a tightly knit Gaelic community lived in a cluster of *bothans*. They had to work very hard to survive, the menfolk fishing offshore in all weathers, and the womenfolk with their *trichuram*, or three tasks: *paisti, pratai agus truscar* (children, potatoes and fertiliser). Fertilising the potato crop involved the back-breaking task of drawing up sea-weed from the shore, mixing it with sand and the contents of the privy and compost heap, and spreading the mixture on the land.

Today there are no mud cabins to be seen, and although a few of the cottages are thatched, they all have a look of solidity, and some show an air of prosperity. The little potato patches, so well manured in the old days, are now mostly lawns; Gaeltacht grants have taken away the necessity.

Beyond the old part of Ballinagoul there is a procession of bungalows, every one of them different, as if similarity was a mortal sin. Pebbledash and tiles, bricks and slates; it is a pity more care was not taken by the planning officer concerned to ensure some element of continuity. Set well back from the road is the house of Liam Clancy (a member of the Clancy Brothers singing group), a substantial building with steeply pitched slated roofs reaching nearly to the ground.

Before long we reached our goal for the day — Ring Post Office, where we were to await the bus back to Ardmore to collect our car. We enquired there about accommodation for the night. Mrs Maher in 'Helvick View', just down the road, was recommended, and we decided to call there when we came back from Ardmore. As we sat on the wall opposite the Post Office, the sun finally burned its way through and bathed us with warmth. Across Dungarvan harbour the tops of the Comeragh Mountains to the north appeared, floating on a sea of fog, like King Kong's island in the movie. Within minutes the whole bay and the coastline to the north-east, with its dark mountain backdrop, were revealed, a most memorable sight to see.

When the bus came, we hopped down from the wall, and I left the seat of my trousers adhering to a sharp stone! So with one hand carrying my knapsack and the other preserving my modesty, and with Teresa following closely behind racked with laughter, we boarded Bus Eireann for the trip back to Ardmore.

In less than two hours we were back in Ring, parking outside 'Helvick View', one of two bungalows side by side bearing the Bord Failte sign. Mrs Bridget Maher welcomed us and showed us to a room that indeed did have a view of Helvick, and a panorama of the rest of Dungarvan harbour thrown in for good measure.

Now equipped with transport, we decided on the Moorings in Dungarvan for our evening meal, a waterside pub and restaurant that had been highly recommended. It had a comfortable atmosphere, its dark panelled walls decorated with fishing nets and glass cases displaying stuffed sea birds. It also had an unexpected but unmistakably affluent clientele, probably executives from Dungarvan's two larger industries, Waterford Crystal and Waterford Co-Op. The cosmopolitan flavour of their repartee seemed light years from the rural surroundings we had been immersed in a short few hours before.

Thirty-five miles of my coastwalk were now completed, and ninety remained before Waterford bridge. Before proceeding much further I could look forward to exploring the town of Dungarvan, a town I had passed through many times, but rarely paused to enjoy.

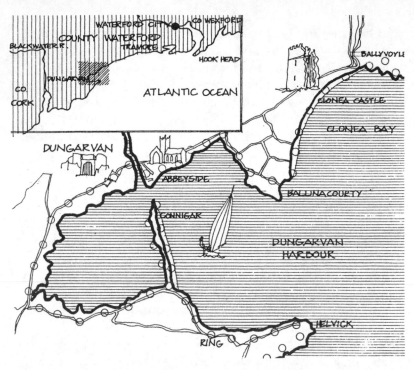

RING TO DUNGARVAN

When I left Ring with Teresa on a fine morning to walk to Dungarvan, the town was only three miles away as the crow flies, but our journey would be a full eight miles around the bay, including following the Cunnigar, a long sand spit, out to its tip and back again. The Cunnigar, from the Gaelic *coinigear* or rabbit warren, extends across the tidal mud flats of the bay from Helvick Head to within a few hundred yards of the centre of Dungarvan town. The wives of the Ballinagoul fishermen used to take fish into Dungarvan to sell by this route, saving three or four miles, crossing the narrow water barrier at low tide with the baskets of fish on their heads. The danger of them drowning in the attempt led to a campaign in the 1880s to build a proper road and bridge connection at a cost of £10,000. Although it received a lot of support, it failed to get the financial backing.

Another scheme was hatched earlier in the 1880s to build a causeway connecting the Cunnigar to Dungarvan, with a view to reclaiming the sloblands on the inland side, about 1,250 acres of land. A canal was envisaged at the Helvick end to drain the streams that run into the slobs. The cost of this scheme was estimated at £14,500, which even in those times could not have been a fortune, and environmental issues would not have put anyone off, so I wonder why it was not carried out.

Today the Cunnigar is a valuable wildlife sanctuary and a marvellous place for those who like a good bracing walk or a jog in the fresh sea air.

As we left the public road and set off along the sands, we could see Dungarvan in the distance, looking in the early morning sun and heat haze like a southern Mediterranean town, the angular planes of gables and facades picked out in a pinkish tone.

A stream runs out through the middle of the Cunnigar for a few hundred yards before it drains into the sands of the beach. Sand martins and swallows circled a pond on the stream's route, dipping down in turn to sweep across the water's surface, hoovering up the clouds of flies. Out on the beach two shelducks waddled along in the company of a small flock of oystercatchers waiting for the tide to go out.

The sixty-foot long ribs of an old wreck protruded from the mud about a hundred yards offshore on the landward side of the peninsula; it must have been tossed into this inner lagoon and wrecked by a violent storm.

About halfway down the Cunnigar, we came to stone walls and the ruins of a number of stone buildings, the shelter of which had encouraged the growth of bushes and small stunted trees. There are extensive grassy meadows on the landward side of the peninsula as it broadens, where a sizable herd of cattle grazes. A fresh water spring, surrounded like a desert oasis with great tufts of palm-like grass, provides a good watering place for the cows and the large population of rabbits that live here. In places, the tightly cropped grass left by the cattle, and finished by the rabbits, allowed extensive clumps of thrift or sea pinks to establish themselves.

On the seaward side farther on, the sand dunes have been lofted to a height of about thirty feet, and the marram grass echoed to the warnings of blackcaps as we made our way through. On the shingle at the water's edge, a host of birds rested — cormorants with their wings hung out to dry, oystercatchers all turned as one into the wind, and picking their way between them a flock of turnstones, tirelessly upending every pebble they could find to expose tiny shore creatures to eat.

About three-quarters of an hour after we had set out along the Cunnigar, we reached the end of the point, only a couple of hundred yards from the gable of the church at Abbeyside in Dungarvan. A small sailing dingy, steered by a lone man, came out from the harbour and tacked neatly towards the open bay, the sea slapping against her side as she heeled over, grabbing the wind. The straining mainsail hurried her along, in and out between the buoys, and then effortlessly through the riptide which tore the water in a line between the point of the sandspit and the mainland.

It was strange to be so close and yet at the same time so remote from the centre of a busy town. We sat on a little sandy knoll where clumps of waxy sea holly grew, some of it bearing clusters of shocking pink cinnabar moths, and listened to the faint sound of the hustle and bustle of Dungarvan. Sea holly is a plant that is slowly disappearing from our coastlines, and with it will go the moths and other insects it supplies with nectar. Linnaeus said that the plant's young shoots are good to eat, and when blanched are only slightly inferior to asparagus. A couple of hundred years ago a sweetmeat was made from its roots mixed with egg yolks and malmsey, and it was taken to 'strengthen the back'. For centuries young married women in Britain wore sea holly as a charm to ensure their husbands' fidelity. Today many of the beaches and seashores where it grows are threatened by overuse at holiday time. The pessimistic side of me supposed that a bridge eventually will be built to the Cunnigar, to allow everyone in their cars to clutter up the sandhills while they read their Sunday newspapers, but the optimistic side felt sure that if the Cunnigar survived the 1980s, it had a guaranteed future.

We set off back to the mainland, walking this time along the beach on the seaward side. The coastline from the base of the

Cunnigar, around the shores of the bay to Dungarvan, consists of mud flats with numerous rivulets and streams running into them, and since it would have been extremely difficult to negotiate these, we decided to take the road instead, which follows the shore about a hundred yards inland. Walking westwards through the townland of Gortnadiha, we passed Gortnadiha House, built as if on a natural rockery planted with lush alpine plants and palms. Across the road was a little meadow valley laid out with beehives, conforming in every way to Yeats's 'bee-loud glade'. A cottage we passed was decorated with cockleshells and coloured glass, one of the only examples of real individualism we found on the Helvick peninsula.

Walking on main roads never appeals to me normally, but at least the stretch along the shores of the Blackwater towards Piltown had considerable scenic attraction to dilute the terror of traffic! The main road into Dungarvan had little of this, except when it crossed the Brickey river, where we watched a pair of herons 'peer and pounce', and passed some fine stone-built farm-houses at Newtown. Still, it was with some relief that we passed through the usual suburban defences that modern towns surround themselves with, and entered Dungarvan.

Dungarvan today is a prosperous place, bustling in that relaxed way of rural towns. Even the great improvements that were carried out here in the early nineteenth century by the Dukes of Devonshire (mainly to increase the value of their holdings in County Waterford) had ceased to impress by the time *Murray's Handbook for Travellers in Ireland* was published in 1866, describing Dungarvan as 'a seaport containing very little of interest and an immense deal of dirt. . . .'

Probably originally a fishing village and a Scandinavian trading post, the place is first mentioned in the annals when the Norman, Raymond le Gros, commandeered its fleet of fishing boats to take plunder back to Wales after a raid on Lismore in 1173. Contrary winds drove them into a fleet of Cork Danes and a vigorous skirmish took place; Norman history records a victory for le Gros, while the other side suggests that the Corkmen brought most of the valuables back to the Lee.

We arrived in the main square of Dungarvan on a sunny after-

noon, relieved to be finished with the long straight road in from
the west, but determined to have a good look around the town
before putting our feet up and taking refreshment.

Dungarvan's central square and the streets leading off it were
laid out as part of the modernisation of the town and port carried
out by the Duke of Devonshire early in the nineteenth century.

The simplicity and quietly comfortable scale of the original square has been maintained to the present day, and even the ubiquitous, but thankfully few, plastic and neon signs have failed to distract from it. The ambience of the place has been likened by Michael Gough, a distinguished town-planner, to the Place Vendôme in Paris.

Leading off the square are the town's main streets, the nicest of which are those that do not take the through-traffic between Waterford and Cork. We wandered down towards the quays along a street where some of the older shops have extremely narrow one-window frontages that one would expect to find in older towns. A network of narrow stone-flagged laneways, some with their old gas lamps still intact, connect the larger streets. Walking along one of these lanes towards the old quays, we were delighted to come across the massive stone ramparts of Dungarvan Castle, growing out of a substantial round tower that must have been more than forty feet high.

I was surprised to find the castle in such good order; most of what I had read about it had prepared me for sections of ruined masonry that could just be identified between the more recent buildings. The reality is the opposite. From the laneway the castle positively towers over all, looking as if its seven-hundred-year-old walls will long outlive those of the more recent buildings around it. It was sad to see, however, what was once the symbol of Dungarvan's economic importance, so neglected.

One of a series of Norman fortifications initiated by Prince John during his visit to Ireland in 1185, it was completed in time to provide accommodation for him during his next visit to Ireland, as King, some years later. Like most Irish castles, it has endured a litany of sieges, surrenders and burnings over the centuries. Its last siege could be said to have been during 1921, when strong republican forces had the town effectively surrounded. Incoming dispatches for the Black and Tans, then using the castle as a barracks, had to be dropped by an RAF aircraft from Cork, causing great excitement amongst the townsfolk. The last burning came during the withdrawal of occupying anti-Treaty forces in the face of a superior Free State army nearly two years later.

At the end of the laneway we walked out onto the old Quays

of Dungarvan, which except for a few pleasure craft have been empty of vessels for a number of years. Dungarvan was for many years a busy fishing port due to its proximity to the Nymph Bank, a fish-rich region of the continental shelf extending westwards to Cape Clear. The bank was discovered in the early 1700s by a fisherman named Doyle, who, during a series of expeditions to the area, filled his boat Galilean-style with an abundance of cod, ling and hake. Doyle carefully plotted the location of the area to enable him to return again and again, but he failed to discover its western limit, which was thought to extend as far as Newfoundland.

A considerable amount of trade passed through Dungarvan in the nineteenth century, particularly after the Duke of Devonshire had invested in the development of the port and had stonebuilt quays constructed. However, shipping began to decline at the beginning of the twentieth century, and today only the shiny cast-iron bollards lining the quays, inscribed with the names of their makers and dating from between 1884 and the early 1990s, remind the visitor of the past.

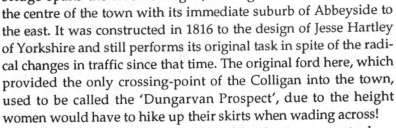

At the inner end of the harbour a fine bridge spans the river Colligan, linking the centre of the town with its immediate suburb of Abbeyside to the east. It was constructed in 1816 to the design of Jesse Hartley of Yorkshire and still performs its original task in spite of the radical changes in traffic since that time. The original ford here, which provided the only crossing-point of the Colligan into the town, used to be called the 'Dungarvan Prospect', due to the height women would have to hike up their skirts when wading across!

Turning seawards and passing the Moorings restaurant where we had eaten the previous evening, we came again upon the ramparts of the castle bursting through some tatty warehouses onto the quayside. Down a nearby laneway and almost obscured by derelict buildings, we found the much altered twin-towered gateway to the castle, which I remembered seeing photographs of, some with 'redcoat' sentries standing guard, and others taken later showing IRA guards in trenchcoats. It will really be a shame if the people of Dungarvan do not take serious measures to ensure that this castle, one of the south coast's most substantial relics, is preserved.

Across the road from the castle entrance is a blocked-up gothic-arched doorway of very weathered cut sandstone, thought by some to be the door to a church founded by St. Garvan in the seventh century.

The old Market House further on has been reconstructed and turned appropriately into a museum and library; a plaque proclaims that it was reopened in 1984 by the writer Molly Keane, who lives in nearby Ardmore. Unfortunately we did not get to see Dungarvan's museum, because for some reason Saturday afternoon was not included in its opening hours.

Down another intriguing narrow laneway we again came out to the quayside, near a limestone plaque on a wall,

TO COMMEMORATE
THE BRAVERY OF THE MEN
WHO VOLUNTEERED TO MAN THE
LIFEBOAT AND RESCUED SEVEN
OF THE CREW OF THE MORESBY
WRECKED IN DUNGARVAN HARBOUR
ON CHRISTMAS EVE 1895

The inscription takes up only half the space on the stone slab, and I wondered had it been planned to inscribe names; maybe because of the controversy that occurred over the affair, it was decided to let sleeping dogs lie.

The *Moresby* story contains an element of mystery, and some old folk in Dungarvan are still sensitive about being asked about the incident, although it happened nearly a hundred years ago.

Shortly before Christmas 1895 the *Moresby*, a 1,155 ton sailing vessel, departed from the port of Cardiff in Wales with a cargo of coal for South America. Rounding Carnsore Point a vicious winter storm blew up, which kept the captain and the crew of twenty-two very busy. After fighting the storm for two days, during which gusting gales had torn some of her sails, the *Moresby* entered Dungarvan Bay. The captain was apparently disorientated, and thought he was entering Cork Harbour.

When a schooner sailing ahead of them went aground on Clonea Strand, the *Moresby* was turned about to avoid the same fate, and in the manoeuvre her remaining sails were shredded. Having lost steerage way, the captain ordered the anchor to be dropped, thinking he could ride out the storm.

Those on shore, however, knew the *Moresby* was in trouble, and the Ballinacourty lifeboat was launched, braving the waves and wind to cross the bay to rescue the stranded seamen. When they arrived alongside the *Moresby*, the captain had decided they

were out of any danger, and declined to be rescued. The peril the lifeboat crew had faced getting to the *Moresby*, and the tenor of the communications between them and the *Moresby*'s crew may have had a bearing on the situation that arose later. The lifeboat returned to shore, and the lifeboatmen returned to their homes.

That night, however, before repairs to the Moresby had been completed, the storm blew up again, with renewed ferocity. The force of the breakers rolling into the bay parted the anchor chains and the *Moresby* was blown helplessly before the wind. At this stage the captain must have been frightened (he had his wife and child aboard), because he ordered distress flares to be sent up.

It was now the early hours of Christmas Eve, and when the Ballinacourty lifeboat cox summoned his crew, they refused to come.

Meanwhile the *Moresby* was driven into the shallows of the Whitehouse Bank, which extends from Helvick Head parallel to the Cunnigar across the bay to the outlet of the Colligan river, and there she went aground.

Breeches buoy equipment was brought from the Helvick Coastguard Station down the Cunnigar and set up, but they failed to get a line aboard the vessel, whose occupants now hung in the rigging awaiting rescue. A volunteer crew was eventually raised for the lifeboat, but before they could effect a rescue, heavy seas rolled the *Moresby* on her side, scattering her crew into the sea. The tide was falling, and most of them, including the captain, his wife and child, were swept out to sea, the volunteer lifeboat arriving in time to rescue only seven, two of whom later died.

The almost forgotten plaque on the wall facing out over Dungarvan Harbour and its emotional message do not hint at the fury of the storm, the bravery of the volunteers, or the despair of those who drowned far out in the bay that Christmas Eve.

Up around the corner in the extensive Protestant graveyard, we found the mass grave of most of the *Moresby*'s victims, covered by a simple stone. Nearby, another gravestone stands with the inscription:

Alls Well
In Loving Memory of Joseph Dean son of Peter
Thomas and Sarah Middleton Dean who was wrecked
off the ship Moresby on Christmas Eve 1895 in
his nineteenth year

The Protestant church, built in 1831, stands beside the ruined gable of another structure, said to be the remains of a church destroyed by Cromwell. If this is so, it would have been a church of unusual proportions, and I do not think I have seen anywhere else in Ireland a similar arrangement of windows, which are circular with a diameter of a few feet, and number five in all.

We crossed the Colligan river to Abbeyside, the 'other side of town', and walked out along the quays to St Mary's Church, a nineteenth-century structure built beside and over part of the ruins of the original abbey, on the shore of the bay. The abbey was founded in the thirteenth century by the McGraths, chieftains of west Waterford, and was occupied by the Eremites of St. Augustine. The recent church is rather a dull gothic design, but it incorporates the sixty-foot tower of the original abbey, complete with its bell. Some of the tombstones in the adjoining graveyard look as if they have been recycled; one, in particular, has an unusual cross deeply incised on its reverse.

Walking in the streets nearby we were surprised to come upon an ordinary suburban bungalow, whose walls and garden were lavishly decorated with cockleshells and pieces of china. It was a marvellous sight, so unexpected and incongruous in its surroundings; on its own somewhere in the countryside it would be easier to assimilate. Thousands upon thousands of shells had been used, together with dishes, bowls, statuettes, aspidistra vases and all kinds of ornaments to make a visual extravaganza. Along the top of the walls, framed in scallop shells, Canadian Mounties joined dogs, Victorian ladies and mantelpiece cats to crown the display, many of the individual pieces looking to my inexperienced eye as if they would fetch a respectable price in an antique shop. Down the side passage we could see that the back garden and the high stone wall behind it were similarly decorated.

This magnum opus was carried out by a seaman who collected

shells from every country he visited, and applied them to his garden walls to display them. Over the years the display grew, augmented by colourful china, and after his death his widow carried on. I found out later that the place is becoming a tourist attraction, and I am not surprised; it is a wonderful piece of eccentricity.

Leaving the 'Shell House' behind, we returned across the bridge to the Moorings for rest and refreshment. We had walked upwards of eight miles from Ring, completing forty-five miles of the coastwalk.

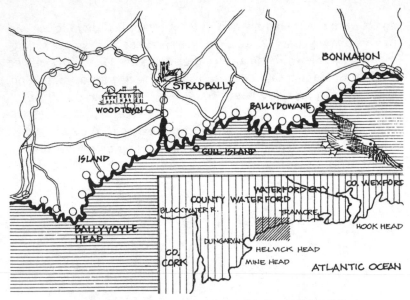

DUNGARVAN TO BUNMAHON

In comparison to the warm sunny arrival into Dungarvan, my departure was made on an overcast morning that brought heavy May showers with monotonous regularity. Teresa was unable to get away from Dublin this time, but I was glad that an old friend, Jim O'Callaghan, came to accompany me for the next stretch to Bunmahon. Although, like myself, Jim has lived most of his adult life in Dublin, he was born and reared in County Meath, and retains a close affinity with things rural.

Leaving Dungarvan's square, we crossed the Duke of Devonshire's bridge over the Colligan and picked up a path that followed the disused railway line from Waterford, passing inland of Abbeyside. This linear park is a great amenity, a kind of sunken promenade with grass banks reaching steeply up to suburban houses on each side.

We followed the pathway through the outskirts of the town and out to the northern side of Dungarvan Harbour, where the old railway line crosses the mud flats of the Spit Bank, then covered with the waters of a high tide, on an embankment. There is nothing more miserable than starting a day's walking in heavy rain, but our depression was considerably relieved by our surroundings, as we strode out as if across the sea on a narrow neck of land. The sight of two shelducks rising from the reeds nearby and circling us in perfect formation further dispelled our poor spirits.

At the end of the causeway, where the railway again meets land, there is a pretty stone-built cottage which used to be a signalman's station. Jim and I had been discussing the railway line, which we thought had been an extension of the old Fishguard-Rosslare-Waterford line, and we called in to enquire of the occupants when the line had ceased to be used. The door was ajar, and inside a kind-faced middle-aged lady sat in an armchair saying her rosary. I expected her to jump out of her skin when she looked up and saw these two wet creatures at her door, but she smiled almost as if she was expecting us, and blessing herself, put her beads away and came out to us.

'Oh, the railway has been closed for donkeys' years,' she told us in response to our query. 'It was one of the first of the small ones to go. The town had lean times and then the big factory came along and gave lots of work, particularly to the young people. For a while it was marvellous for those working in it; they had outings galore. You know, when they were doing overtime they had their dinner sent out by the hotel!'

She laughed at the idea of it.

'Many's the young lad bought his house and married and settled on the strength of it, but suddenly it was gone. It's an awful eyesore now.'

She was referring to the ill-fated Pffiesser plant, which through the sixties and seventies had marked the sky over Dungarvan Harbour with a tall, ugly column of white smoke.

Leaving this friendly woman, we headed out along the shore towards Ballincourty. This southeastern shore of the Ballincourty peninsula is called the Gold Coast; I'm not sure why, but the opulence of some of the residences we saw there would be reason enough. I say some of the residences, because here and there, sandwiched between fine houses in lush landscaped garden settings, there are run-down derelict cottages, as if to remind the well-off of the other side of life.

The Gold Coast Lounge Bar and Restaurant stands beside a well-designed, unobtrusive holiday home development planned on a crescent overlooking Dungarvan Harbour; in more favourable weather, it would be a great place for a holiday. At a little stone-built harbour we had to follow the road inland, briefly, to avoid the greens of Dungarvan Golf Club.

After about fifteen minutes, we came suddenly upon the closed gateway to the shut-down Pffiesser plant. What a sight it was! A great hulking, corroding building clad in asbestos panelling, some of which looked as if it had been blasted away by shellfire, revealing the grim dark interior. All around stood gantries, cranes and hoists, like mechanical monsters waiting to feed on a dying giant. It is an ideal location for films about the aftermath of World War III! I wondered how much tax-payers' money lay scattered about this dreadful scene, and at the expense of the railway spur that was built to link the factory with the national network.

Out on the point, beyond the factory ruins, is Ballincourty Lighthouse, erected at the request of the 'Merchants of Ballincourty' in 1851. It was built from stone extracted from a limestone quarry nearby, from where in the last century considerable quantities were quarried and shipped up and down the coast, for slaking or building purposes.

Not much farther on we came to the shore once again, where the sea, with some wind behind it, was breaking against the ragged and dramatically twisted limestone formations of Ballincourty Point. Turning north along the rocks, we headed down Clonea strand, stretching ahead of us into the misty rain. At the far end, nearly three miles away, Ballyvoyle Head was barely visible, while halfway down the beach the gaunt outline of Clonea Castle loomed.

Clonea Castle was a most precarious ruin, perched on rocks at the back of the strand and severely undermined by the sea. Within months of our passing by, it was demolished due to its dangerous condition.

The castle was owned from the late eighteenth century to the 1920s by the MacGwire family. Walter MacGwire had spent a number of years in India working for the East India Company under Warren Hastings and is reputed to have brought an Indian woman home with him to share his retirement in Ireland. One of Walter's sons, Richard, achieved a short-lived fame in Dublin in 1785 for his prowess as an aviator.

Richard and some of his fellow students from Trinity College were part of a large crowd that had collected on the outskirts of Dublin to watch a famous balloonist named Crosbie make an ascent. For some reason, there wasn't sufficient gas to get Crosbie off the ground, so MacGwire, being light-framed, as well as young and foolish, offered to have a try, and was accepted.

The lines were cast off and up he rose to the oohs and aaahs of the admiring crowd high over Georgian Dublin, where the wind caught the flimsy aircraft and began to blow it eastwards towards the sea. Aviation was a young science at the time, and no method had been devised to control a balloon in flight, so our Richard could do nothing but hang on tight and await developments. His friends raced after the balloon on horseback, across the Liffey and on out towards Clontarf as it drifted over Dublin Bay.

At this stage the balloon decided to lose height, and before long it deposited Richard (who at this stage must have been sincerely regretting his impetuosity) into the Irish Sea. He started to swim for shore and was just beginning to tire when his faithful friends arrived to rescue him in a boat they had commandeered at

Clontarf. They took the hero back into Dublin, to the acclaim of the crowds who had awaited news of the amateur aeronaut. The following Sunday he was invited to Dublin Castle to be knighted by the Lord Lieutenant. He was the talk of the city, and one of the newspapers carried an ode to him which began

> Oh, for a muse of fire
> Which would ascend and emulate MacGwire

A picture was painted of the epic rescue from Dublin Bay, of which there is an engraved reproduction in the National Gallery of Ireland. Richard MacGwire is not recorded as having flown again, and after this high point at the beginning of his career, he is said to have joined the Army, and disappeared into obscurity.

One of the last members of the MacGwire family left Clonea House and gardens, the 'pleasure grounds', and 180 acres to the Society of St. Vincent de Paul Society, because, it is said, it was the only really Christian organisation he knew. He lies buried under a grove of trees in the gardens of Clonea House, just behind where the castle stood.

In the grass beside the castle we came across two ravens hopping around vigorously, apparently unable to fly. We could not see any obvious disability other than what seemed to be a thin oily coating on their feathers. Another raven, however, was circling overhead, keeping an eye on things, so we finally decided they were newly fledged young from a nest in the castle wall above, and had failed to prolong their first flight. Leaving the birds in the care of their watchful parent, we hoped they would not be found by a roaming dog before they had mastered the air.

I am sure Clonea beach is a paradise in the sunshine, but the rain there on the day we passed made it a miserable scene. An extensive flock of lesser blackbacked gulls, lining the water's edge as if in a catatonic depression with the weather, hardly bothered to make way for us as we passed. At the east end of the beach we came to a sea-wall that would not have been out-of-place at Omaha Beach on D-Day, holding back the cliffs behind from burying the remains of numerous washing machines, fridges and other detritus, including an old Morris Minor, littering the foreshore.

Here, just west of where the land rises up to the cliffs of Ballyvoyle Head and the Daligan river empties into the sea, we decided to attempt to raise our severely dampened spirits by lighting a fire and cooking a bit of lunch. We searched the high water mark in vain for adequate dry kindling before trying to light a pathetic pyre of damp sticks and paper. Hunched over the epicentre trying to provide some shelter, we struck match after match, applying them unsuccessfully until the matchbox was empty, before giving up and retreating in disarray. As we moved off we discovered that somehow, somewhere, during our efforts we had got sticky oily tar on our waterproof trousers, anoraks and knapsacks.

We crossed the Daligan by a fine old three-arched bridge near which a limekiln of equal age was built in against the cliff. As we reached the other side of the river, a watery sun broke through the low clouds and the rain simultaneously reduced to a light drizzle. We ascended from the beach on to the landward end of Ballyvoyle Head by way of a narrow boreen, with high ditches decorated with masses of violets, speedwell, primroses and white and pink thrift whose perfume transcended the damp air. Passing a beautifully sited whitewashed summer cottage, we were once again in the fields, climbing along the flank of the headland. Dropping down briefly to cross a road leading to a tiny cove, we climbed the other side of a little valley to reach the crown of Ballyvoyle Head, 238 feet above sea level.

Around Ballyvoyle all the fields are bounded with well-built stone walls, the stone no doubt coming from what is said to have been a Fitzgerald castle, the remains of the bawn of which we came across perched on the edge of the 200-foot cliffs, measuring some forty metres square.

A couple of hundred yards inland, in a townland called Island, can be found the remains of one of the biggest stone forts in south-east Ireland. It is so extensive, and its walls are so disguised with gorse, hawthorn and briars, that it can be easily mistaken for just another field. Within the fort is an ogham stone marking a grave.

On a previous visit to the area looking for the fort, I met the landowner, Thomas Clancy, who had followed my car down the muddy boreen that passed his house to see if I had gone astray. A sturdy old gentleman with a stout stick, he was most helpful when he found out what I was after.

'Last Easter twelve months two women came here,' he told me as he took me across the fields. 'One was from Trinity College, Dublin, and the other from Belfast, and they gave me a bit of reading on the grave.'

We stooped to get under a strand of electric fence across a gap in a hedge, and I found myself standing in the roughly circular fort, its overgrown walls at under five feet in height, looking similar to the surrounding field boundaries. The structure has no dramatic features: only the size of the stones that make up the wall and its extent give an idea of what it must have been like when complete.

Thomas made his way across to the western side and showed me the ogham stone, which originally stood in the centre of the fort, and now lies in the grass. It is a five feet long piece of schist, cracked through the middle and with unmistakable ogham markings along its arrises.

'A man that was here a long time ago dug it up and brought it home to make a lintel over a door,' Thomas told me, tapping the stone with his stick. 'And when he did that, he didn't have luck; he was losing cattle and everything. The priest told him to bring the stone back if he wanted peace. He did bring it back, but he broke it by mistake.'

Thomas took me to his house and showed me an envelope marked 'The King's Grave', containing a handwritten note on the ogham stone written by 'P. Ni Chatain'. The note indicated that the inscription on the stone translated as 'The grave of Cunnetas the Son of the descendant of Neta Segamanas'. Deo Segomo was apparently a Gaulish God, suggesting a connection between this place and Gaul, and the note dated the stone from about the first century B.C.

Further east, Jim and I came across yet another relic of former days, a remarkably well-preserved promontory fort, a needle of rock extending out and away from the cliffs, with a tenuous attachment to the mainland. The weather had by now become far more civilised, so we decided we were entitled to a stop. We made our way through a narrow gap in a ditch, across a thin causeway with cliffs on either side, and out on to the promontory, about a third of an acre covered with tussocks of thick springy grass. Shapes in the grass could have been concealing the remains of buildings, and indeed we found that a neat three feet square hole had been recently excavated in the middle of the space and wondered had they, treasure hunters or archaeologists, found anything of note.

Jim had been husbanding a flask of boiling water through all our morning misery, waiting for a suitable moment to make coffee, and we agreed that now was the time. We sat on the well-upholstered ground, our feet in the excavation (having first checked that there were no highly decorated gold Celtic jewellry on the bottom) and luxuriated in the preparation and consumption of a delicious South American blend. Those few moments perched high above the sea, with the aroma of coffee wafting on the clear air, rank amongst the most memorable of the whole coastwalk.

The shore line along this coast is almost completely inaccessible; in only a few locations did we spot a precarious pathway heading steeply down the cliffs. No doubt some of these would have been used by smugglers, although it was difficult to imagine goods of any bulk being brought up such paths from the shore two hundred feet below.

Not far west of Stradbally as we dropped down into a valley to cross a stream, a pair of choughs flew past us and gave a spectacular display of aerobatics before disappearing over the cliffs, calling plaintively to each other. On the west bank of the stream the ground was thick with primroses, and the first sprouting of plants that I wildly guessed were early purple orchids. The appearance of flowers again was very welcome, because we found that most of the fields to the west of Stradbally consisted of heavily fertilised dark-green fodder grass, not only boring because of its lack of variety of herbs and wildlife but, when thick, very tiring underfoot.

About two hours after leaving Clonea Strand, we rounded the western side of Stradbally Cove and picked up a fine pathway that gently descended between banks of primroses to the beach.

Stradbally Cove is quite narrow, stretching almost half a mile from the road to the tide at its lowest point. The cliff walkway brought us down to the road past an old limekiln. Turning right and crossing a bridge over the Tay river, we passed the back gates to the Woodhouse demesne and started uphill on the last few hundred yards into Stradbally village.

Stradbally is a beautiful picturesque village, with a number of traditional thatched cottages and small late-Georgian houses, against a rich backdrop of mature trees. If it were a little less scattered, and the houses more closely grouped, it would be my ideal village.

As usual, a visit to the village church in the village is all that one needs to find out which are the main landowning families in the area. An ordinary exterior conceals an austere and simply proportioned space, decorated in a quiet, dignified way in creams and dark browns. The most frequent name on the walls of the church is Beresford. So often does it appear, one would be excused for thinking that this was their private chapel, and I suppose in a way it was.

The original landlords in this area were the Uniackes, but the lands came into the Beresford ownership by marriage in the early 1800s. The Beresfords were obviously loyal servants of the Crown, since almost all of those mentioned on commemoration plaques held army ranks, and one sad inscription honours a Richard Beresford who died in Calcutta in 1869, aged twenty-nine, after a short illness.

Another plaque mentions a daughter of Edward MacGwire of Clonea Castle who must surely have been a descendant of the 'balloon man'.

Beside the church are the remains of a much-altered and extended older building, its nave filled with a large number of interesting grave slabs. A number of mausoleums stand in the graveyard, one of which, crudely built, uses finely cut decorative stones vandalised from an earlier structure, perhaps the old church itself.

Jim and I walked up the main street to the nearest pub to quench a growing thirst. The Cove Bar is one of two pubs in

Stradbally, both on High Street, said to have been a main thoroughfare in medieval times. Slipping in through its narrow doors, we shrugged off our knapsacks and ordered a couple of pints. It must not be a common sight to see two men no longer in the bloom of youth walking about the countryside with knapsacks on their backs. There was a curiosity about what we were up to, and we were soon in conversation with the friendly proprietor, about the coast we had walked and County Waterford in general. The landlord told us that Stradbally was a quiet place, with a very small holiday population, and although it had been a centre for boy-scouts for years, they had ceased to come in numbers since Woodhouse Estate, where their traditional camping ground had been, had passed out of the Beresford family.

We enquired of our landlord about accommodation in Stradbally, and a Mrs Connors of Park House was recommended, so after making a phone call to check, we left the Cove Bar to find our bed for the night. We were told that the Connors house was a few hundred yards up the road. This gross underestimate should have warned us about a kink or trait in the rural Waterford person's distance-measuring ability; either their units of distance were some ancient and long-lost interpretation of the terms 'yards' or 'miles', or they just never thought much about such things. We were to pay heavily for this before the night was out.

Passing an old crumbling handball alley, we came, after half-a-mile, to the old village hall, beyond which a sign proclaimed 'Park House 200 yards' and indicated a left turn. After what felt like four hundred yards, we came to a long drive with another sign stating 'Park House'. The drive itself was, I am sure, almost half a mile long and we were footsore when we entered a thick screen of conifers and finally found Park House nestling in a bird-loud glade.

Mrs Connors, a dark, well built woman, greeted us and showed us to our rooms, which were neat and comfortable. She had not wanted to feed us when we rang, but we persuaded her to do so, and after changing we sat down to a welcome dinner.

We decided to return to the village for a drink after dinner, but when Mrs Connors mentioned that there was a bar nearer than the village, it seemed like a better idea. She directed us across the fields and down the road, saying it was about half a mile altogether. Almost an hour later we were still walking when the rain started to come down, quickly followed by the dark, black as it can only be in a country place. Thinking eventually we had misheard the directions, we asked at a cottage door and were told, yes, we were on the right road for the pub, it was just half a mile farther on! We were beginning to feel as if we were in the 'Twilight Zone' when we finally came upon the place.

It was a cosy little pub, and from the ages of the clientele, which ran from seven to seventy, it appeared to be the local community centre. Over our pints we asked the landlord what was the name of the river we had crossed on our way from Mrs Connors. He told us it was the Dalligan, and that it entered the sea a mile and a half further south! We thought this to be a bit of an exaggeration, but a later check on my map showed his estimate to be right, so we had in our search for a quiet pint circled back around to within half an hour of the end of Clonea strand!

It was raining heavily as we started back to Park House, and although we had our waterproofs on, we were soaked by the time we arrived. Mrs Connors kindly took our wet gear away to dry, and we chatted for a while in the living room, which had an end wall almost completely covered with red and blue rosettes.

'We're a riding family, all of us,' Mrs Connors explained, 'and we've all won a few gymkhana.'

The following morning it was still raining, and the trees and shrubs around Park House were drooping miserably. We had expressed an interest in seeing the Woodhouse demesne, and Mrs Connors said we could take a short cut through it on our way back to the beach. In spite of our being convinced that we would probably end up back again in Clonea, we left Park House guided by Mrs Connors' daughter, who took us through a series of haggards and down into the wooded demesne.

Deep in the woods Jim and I met the river Tay which we had crossed the day before on our way into Stradbally, so we knew we were on the right track. It was still raining, and with everything dripping, we felt a bit like explorers in the Amazon jungle during the wet season. All around us great trees towered out of a thick lush undergrowth. Some of them were probably planted in the mid eighteenth century when it was recorded that the estate was laid out by the then owner with 152,640 trees of all varieties!

Wild flowers grew in abundance everywhere and exotic trees struggled to compete with vigorous local species. The fresh delicate green leaves of young beeches stood out against the darker tones of the undergrowth, each leaf exactly the same shape and configuration as its neighbour, almost like a repeat pattern painted on a backdrop. These young trees made up a secondary forest nearer the ground than the as yet unleafed canopies of the mature ivy-clad giants towering overhead.

As we walked, the rain ceased, and a cuckoo's clear song echoed through the wood. The sky cleared, and beams of sunlight spotlighted masses of bluebells, violets and new ferns along the pathway, and now and then as we walked, I caught the whiff of wild garlic.

The wood gradually opened to the south and gave way to extensive meadows; altogether this demesne is a beautiful place of contrasts, with meadows, wooded hills and river banks all contributing to the ambience.

The track we followed eventually took us close to the back of Woodhouse, a fine, much-added-to house of indeterminate age, with a little belfry adorning one of the older sections. We eventually passed by the little gate lodge, and reached the public road just behind Stradbally Beach.

At the far side of the road we climbed steeply up through a young beech-wood to a boreen which brought us out towards the cliffs. Reaching the cliff edge, nearly 200 feet above the water, we turned east along a pathway through the gorse and heather. An absolutely tremendous seastack of twisted shale rose up from the base of the cliffs, a Manhattan-like home for large numbers of gulls, guillemots, cormorants and shags.

The end of the large stone wall we had crossed earlier appeared ahead of us at right angles to the cliffs, running to the very edge and even cantilevering over it a little to make sure no-one got by. However, we cut inland a short distance and were able to cross the wall through a breach without difficulty.

The next significant feature offshore was Gull Island, a high flat-topped rock crowned with thick tussocks of grass, and as its name suggested, inhabited by numerous black-backed gulls.

Three-quarters of an hour after leaving Stradbally, we began to descend towards Ballyvooney cove. A clearing in the sky displayed the northern 'corner' of the Comeraghs and Crotty's Rock. There were some new electric fences around the fields here, and when I gave a wire a few quick taps to see if it was live, I received a hell of a kick up my arm and across my chest. The heifers, which had been quietly grazing in the field, all looked up as I let loose a string of expletives as electric as the fence!

We crossed the river that flows into the sea at the stoney Ballyvooney cove and headed uphill again along the cliffs that climbed up towards Ballydowane and Bunmahon. Coming down towards us was a tall, thin man dressed in a navy blue suit of antique cut. He wore a pair of ancient, holed wellingtons into which his trousers were stuffed, and a cap that was many sizes too small. He raised the gnarled hawthorn stick he was carrying in greeting to us and wished us good day.

'You'd want to watch them cliffs ahead there,' he said waving his stick towards the east. 'There's some terrible cave-ins, and ye could end up in the sea. Where're ye headed for?'

We told him we were making for Bunmahon, and asked was it far.

'A couple o' mile, I'd say,' he replied.

'Is it near here that Seanin a'Mounta lived in the old days?' I asked, remembering stories I had heard as a child about Ballyvooney, and seeing the possibility of some local lore in his brown humourous eyes.

'Indeed he did, away over on the hill there. He was a class of a magician, or so they say anyway.' He took a 'dry' pipe out of his pocket and stuck it in the corner of his mouth, looking at us from one to the other to check if we were still interested.

'He would pay a half-a-crown over the counter of Foran's bar in Stradbally for a drink, and after he got his change, the half-crown would turn to a penny! They swore that happened a number of times. He would make a horse stop in the middle of the road by just lookin' at it. He was a strange man, indeed' he said, taking his pipe out of his mouth and spitting strongly over his shoulder.

'A bunch o' men were playin' cards in his place in Rathnaskillogue one night. The candle was going down, so Seanin told the Ace of Hearts to go out to the other room for a new one. Well, the playin' card slithered down off the table and out to the other room while men around the table sat petrified! After a minute or two didn't it come back wrapped around a candle, and Seanin lit it. The bunch o' them left in a hurry! Queer goin's on, alright! Have ye heard of the Hoppin' Ghost?'

What could we do but say we had not, and wait with bated breath!

'That happened near here too,' he said, seeming a bit surprised that we knew nothing about it. He gave another healthy spit over his shoulder.

'On the hill over there,' he pointed with his pipe, 'when I was a young fella a lot of people used see a ghost on the road who hopped along. It got so bad, no-one would go along the road at night and even puttin' salt in your pocket did no good. One night a young fella I knew saw the ghost hoppin' along and shouted at him what was he doin'. The ghost told him that they had tied his big toes together during the wake, for a joke, and never untied them. So the young fella got his knife and cut the string, and the ghost disappeared, and was never seen again! Queer goin's on, alright!' He nodded and nodded as if to emphasise the truth of what he was saying.

'I have to be on my way now,' he said, putting his pipe back into his pocket, and raising his stick in farewell as he walked off down the field, leaving us rooted to the spot, not knowing how to react.

'Watch those cliffs,' he called to us as a parting shot as we turned and continued on our way, wondering had he made up the whole lot on the spot. When we looked back again, we could see his head surmounted by its tiny cap bobbing up and down along the roadway down to Ballyvooney Cove.

At Ballydowane Bay the pathway along the cliff disappears over the precipice in places where great slices of earth and rock have eroded into the battering sea below, so our storyteller was right about the danger. One of the cliffs here is called Faill a'Phluir, or Cliff of Flour, a name that stuck after a schooner was dashed against the rocks below in the nineteenth century, spilling its cargo of flour, and leaving for a few hours the amazing sight of hundreds of yards of pure white cliffs which the people for miles around flocked to see.

On the eastern side of Ballydowane Bay we dropped our knapsacks and sat to take a rest on a spectacular promontory jutting out towards a rock called St. John's Island. Perched so high above the water, we soaked up the sensations of the sea, sun and air while the local fulmars put on an entertaining aerobatic display. Balzac had it right when he wrote: 'We must acknowledge that solitude is a fine thing; but it is a pleasure to have someone to whom we can say that solitude is a fine thing!'

On our way again, we dropped down into a deep valley at Rinnemoe and crossed a stream, before rising up almost 200 feet again to the cliffs. Not far from Rinnemoe we reached what remained of the promontory fort called Illaunobric, now standing apart from the cliffs, lonely and inaccessible. This, it is said, was the citadel of the patriarch of the O'Bric clan in pre-Norman times whose ancient territory extended from Illaunobric to the river Suir and from Credan Head in Waterford harbour to Lismore. There is very little left today of this earth-banked and palisaded homestead, much of it, and the Norman castle that is said to have superseded it, having fallen into the sea over the last few hundred years.

Up to recently, the local people believed that the fort was Danish, and was used by them as base while they raided the surrounding countryside. The field behind the fort, known as Bawn Oilean, was said to be where they used to play sports and practice with their weapons.

A close examination of the cliff faces around Illaunobric will reveal a number of apparent openings or adits, believed by some archaeologists to be Bronze Age copper mines. Certainly mining went on here more recently; a Waterford man named Wise (he obviously was) took a mining lease on these cliffs in the eighteenth century and, over forty years, extracted 'a vast deal of lead and silver' , the silver alone reported to have weighed over seventeen tons.

Farther east we passed Slippery Island which is, like

Illaunobric was really a headland promontory, before the pathway disappeared over the cliffs again and substantial erosion forced us into the fields. We walked eastwards through field after field of thick, nitrogen-fed grass, devoid of any herbs or meadow flowers and heavy and monotonous underfoot. Somewhere along here a rich copper mine, called Transtrelia, was worked in the nineteenth century. I saw no traces of mine buildings which must now make up the many field walls in the area.

After a number of stretches of uncomfortable brambles and gorse, the clifftop path became more continuous, bounded by fragrant banks of violets and sea pinks. All the time as we walked, gulls and fulmars practiced their soaring skills over the cliff edge, joined occasionally by ravens. For someone who is used to seeing ravens in the solitude of the mountains, it is strange to see them sharing the updraughts with a variety of other birds. I have a feeling that the ravens who live by the sea are a little smaller, their plumage not as jet-black, and their 'honk' not as deep as their mountain cousins.

Strangely shaped crags, needles and small islands stand just offshore of the tall cliffs here, some crowned with little pastures of lush grass dotted with gorse bushes. We were delighted to find that two of the biggest, named Gull Island (the third since Youghal) and Shag Island, lived up to their names; a small colony of blackheaded gulls occupied one, and the tussocks of grass on the other were home to a couple of dozen cormorants and shags. During World War I, when imported fertilisers were in short supply, farmers used climb to the top of stacks like these to collect guano.

On the rocks below Gull Island it is said that the remains of a 1600-ton Spanish cargo vessel called the *Civilo Amores* can still be seen at low tide. She lost her rudder during a storm in the winter of 1926 and was unceremoniously dumped high and dry at the cliff bottom. All the crew were saved by breeches buoy, and the local people had oranges, raisins and tinned tomatoes added to their diet for some time after. Even the local pigs seem to have benefited, their usual swill being augmented by tons of long-grained rice, at which the local populace turned up their noses!

Dunabrattin Head was in sight ahead to the east as we started to descend towards the bay of Bunmahon. It was low tide, and the beach looked magnificent below, stretching clean to where the Mahon river crossed it to enter the sea. A young couple walked hand in hand across its extent towards the rising tide of foaming white breakers. A stiff easterly breeze sprang up, its passage across the strand indicated by flurries of fine sand. Along the last of the cliffs, a party of fulmars played on the upcurrents created by the breeze, some of them gliding and hovering within a few feet of us, their webbed feet dropping now and again like an aircraft's airbrakes, and every feather in their wings quivering with the effort of holding the right configuration to achieve the most efficient flight.

And so into the village of Bunmahon, which follows the coast road along the seafront and then uphill and inland. We were taken aback to find Haye's pub closed for renovations; we had been fuelling our energies over the last few miles with the thought of sitting down to a cup of coffee or better as soon as we arrived in Bunmahon. I was sure there were two pubs in the village, but wandering up and down the street we failed to see any of the usual Guinness or Smithwicks signs that would signify its location. At the top of the village, we enquired of two men working on a building site, who looked as if they could appreciate our problem. They directed us back down the village, saying Kirwin's pub was just opposite Hayes. We were surprised and said we had not seen any sign of it.

'You'll see less inside it,' they laughed.

So down the hill again, and sure enough, there was a building that looked as if it could be a pub, but possessing no sign indicating the case. We made our way through the narrow doorway, into near darkness and a not unpleasant smell of oldness. We found ourselves in what looked like a dilapidated living room, with a low counter taking up two sides. Shelves behind the counter held a very limited number of bottles.

We could hear someone moving around in a back room, but no-one appeared until a girl came in from the street and called out 'Sis, are you there?'

Sis materialised suddenly from the dim background, an elderly lady dressed in a number of cardigans and an overcoat. No, there was no coffee, she replied in a surprisingly strong, melodious voice to our request, seeming vaguely disapproving of two men ordering coffee in a pub. The alternative put forward by Jim, two hot whiskeys, was accepted immediately as a bone-fide order and Sis disappeared into the back to put on the kettle.

A low-slung rust brown terrier came hurrying out to us from the back room as if to entertain us while the kettle was boiling, and Sis took down cigarettes for the other customer. Jim and I sat down at a fine old oak dining table, on something that resembled a very long car seat; it seemed leather covered, and it stretched about ten feet along one side of the table, on the centre of which stood a vase with a rich and fresh mixture of wild flowers.

The dog, who possessed the most unlikely name of Kim, got to know us in a few minutes and leapt up into Jim's lap, correctly identifying him as the dog-lover of the two. Sis brought out the hot whiskeys which cost less, or seemed to, than ordinary whiskeys.

I asked Sis about the old mines at Bunmahon, and when they had finally closed.

'They opened again around 1905,' she replied strangely, as if I had missed the first part of her answer, 'but only for eighteen months or so and then went.' The way she put it gave the event a great feel of finality.

'It was an English company, and they built all kinds of strange gadgets around. There were twenty pubs in Bunmahon in the early days, but they were gone before my time and I'm gone eighty. There are only two now.'

She chatted to us about the old days while we finished our drinks, and, vigorously sweeping the floor, bade us a safe journey when we left. Jim and I walked out of Bunmahon village towards the bridge over the Mahon river.

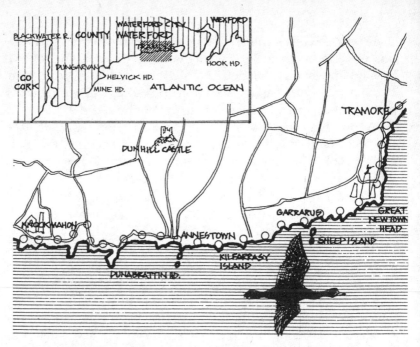

BUNMAHON TO TRAMORE

Mining operations have been going on in Bunmahon since the Bronze Age, when primitive miners with antler scrapers followed the copper veins exposed on the cliff-face inland. During the eighteenth and early nineteenth centuries efforts to follow the increasingly elusive deposits met with limited success before the Mining Company of Ireland, the country's first properly financed and organised mining company, set up operations here in the 1820s.

While previous attempts had lacked the technology and adequate financial backing fully to exploit the ore veins, the Mining Company's operation was on a comparatively enormous scale. Great engine houses were constructed over the shafts, an elaborate system of millraces and water wheels (one of which was forty feet in diameter) were laid out to power the stone-crushers and keep the shafts clear of water, and a small harbour was built to load ships with the ore which was taken to Swansea for smelting. Experienced miners were brought over from Cornwall to carry out the skilled work, and entire local families men, women and children were employed on the surface. At the height of its operations, the Mining Company of Ireland employed up to 1500 people, including children from ten years old.

The mineshafts went down great depths to follow the ore veins, in some cases up to 600 feet below the level of the sea. The miners started their day at 6 am, climbing down to the workfaces by ladder, and working a twelve-hour day in dank, candle-lit conditions before having to climb back out again.

Those who worked on the surface were comparatively well paid, labouring for one shilling and twopence per day in 1840 when a typical farm labourer in the area received four old pence per day with his food, probably a mug of 'blue' or skimmed milk and a couple of salted herrings. Women and children also worked a twelve-hour day, mainly in the dressing sheds where they sorted the ore, hammering off and discarding waste rock.

What had been a tiny village and 'watering place' grew into a town, with twenty-one public houses, two hotels and shops of all kinds. In addition to those who worked directly for the mines and those who provided services for the population, a collection of poor camp followers gathered in Bunmahon, waiting for work and otherwise living off the crumbs from the tables of the better off.

Many of these lived in a shanty town of nearly a hundred single-roomed huts between the main road and the sand dunes, roughly where the caravan park is today. Thirty-nine of these huts housed more than one family, and the overcrowding and poor sanitary conditions must have made the place a hell on earth. During the Great Famine the inhabitants of this shanty town were the first to be affected, and were eventually almost wiped out, only eighteen of the original 129 families surviving.

As always where you find men working long hours of backbreaking labour, the main recreations in Bunmahon were drink, drink and more drink. Every weekend the men went on a binge to forget the drudgery of their lives, and in those days the weekend lasted only from Saturday night to 6 o'clock on Monday morning. Inevitably there were fights and minor riots, and the police were kept busy. Sore heads on Monday mornings meant less productivity in the mines, so the Mining Company joined with the clergy to campaign against the demon drink. A temperance hall was built in 1841 with facilities for tee-totallers' recreation: today it is in use as the Catholic chapel.

A Cornishman named John Pentherick was a manager of the mines in the early days, and from the beginning showed a socialist concern for the workers. He was actively involved in the Repeal Movement, and agitated for more funds to be spent on the education of the poor and workers' children; Daniel O'Connell called him 'a true friend of liberty, a plain straightforward Englishman, a rough English diamond'.

A fellow Englishman, David Doudney, lived in Bunmahon as a minister of the Established Church between 1847 and 1858, and must have been instrumental in transforming the lives of many there. Doudney originally ran a London evangelical publication called the *Gospel Magazine*, which in 1846 raised the considerable sum of £700 for famine relief. He came to Ireland to distribute the Indian meal that the funds had purchased, and, greatly disturbed by what he saw, stayed on to help and do a little missionary work. The local Established Church was impressed by his zeal and energy, and invited him to become a minister. Although it must have been a major career sacrifice for Doudney, he accepted. He was ordained in 1847, and took up the appointment as minister to the parish of Monksland, County Waterford, at the centre of which was the then well-established mining town of Bunmahon.

Bunmahon in 1847 was a tough place in which to live, with overcrowding and food shortages causing great distress. Doudney wrote on his arrival 'one's heart is perfectly sickened in walking through the village itself, and beholding the filth, the wretchedness and the misery that presented itself at every hand'.

The first two years were very difficult, particularly for his wife, who was struggling to raise a large family in a dilapidated rectory. At this point Doudney was offered a post back in England, 'with upwards of 6,000 souls, a church to be built, the funds to be collected under my instrumentality; and an increase in income.' For three months he agonised over the offer, comparing it with his poor circumstances in Bunmahon. 'I am hardly able to meet my daily outlay', he wrote in his diary, 'Lord, what would Thou have me do?"

In the end he stayed on, and was inspired to return to his former profession, printing and publishing. Over a few years he set up a printing house, importing trained printers to teach local boys and began to publish evangelical texts. It was a difficult task, 'considering it was a dark Popish village of about two thousand inhabitants, with merely 100 Protestants (including children)'.

In order to do these things, Doudney turned to the readership of the *Gospel Magazine*, who had been so generous on behalf of Ireland on a previous occasion. Their sponsorship changed things dramatically for him: not only could he afford to purchase printing presses and pay trained printers, but he bought one of the local hotels in which to set up his print shop. The first substantial publication from Bunmahon was Volume One of Gill's *Commentary on the Old and New Testaments*, followed over the next few years by a further five volumes. Each volume had upwards of a thousand pages, and in all 2,250 sets were produced; by any measure an impressive production from 'that dark and desolate village . . . in the midst of such blinded bigotry.' The work involved Doudney for much of his time from 'before daybreak till 9 and 10 at night . . . in addition to preaching sometimes three times on the Sabbath, here at 10 and 3 and at Stradbally, four miles off, at 12.'

Gill's *Commentary* was followed by the printing and mailing at Bunmahon of the *Gospel Magazine*, a phenomenal 15,000 copies per month, and many other religious texts. Having provided employment and training in a skilled trade to a large number of local boys, Doudney now turned his attention to the younger children, and established an Infants School for the Catholic poor.

Sixteen Catholic and three Protestant children, all under seven, attended the first day of the school, and, no doubt attracted by the offer of new clothing and a midday meal, within six months the numbers had risen to 62 children. The Catholic clergy denounced Doudney from the pulpit, and there were threats to excommunicate the Catholic children who attended. Doudney said the catholics would not be encouraged to join his church, but all the children would be taught to read the Bible.

The Agricultural School was set up because Doudney felt that the Irish peasant's 'hereditary and indolent dependence on the potato crop' was the major cause of the Famine, and that such problems could be avoided in the future if a wider range of food crops was adopted. The school therefore concentrated on teaching up-to-date thinking on husbandry, crop rotation and soils, and gave practical experience in the planting of experimental crops to the eighteen or so boys from the Parochial School. In the Embroidery School, set up to give a skill and employment to the girls of the parish, Mrs Doudney took part. The girls were trained to embroider collars, cuffs and sleeves, and within a couple of years the produce of the Bunmahon school was being exported and sold in Nottingham, Tunbridge Wells and London.

In 1858, Doudney, having faced accusations of being a 'Souper', threats to his life and a constant shortage of funds for eleven years, returned to England and today there is no visible trace remaining of his time in Bunmahon.

The mines closed in the 1880s and the bustling town became a sleepy village again. In 1905 the shafts were re-opened and mining work recommenced, only to cease within a year, as politics, business and the price of copper on the international market conspired to starve the venture of funds.

Bunmahon today is a resort village of increasing popularity. Everywhere one looks, the signs of its industrial past can be seen. The land lacks a natural 'lie', but the mounds, stone walls and ruined buildings are now happily overgrown and softened by vegetation and abundant wild flowers, and form a kind of parkland — a natural amenity.

A couple of weeks had passed since Jim O'Callaghan and I had completed the coastwalk as far as Bunmahon, and Teresa rejoined me for the short stretch to the village of Annestown. Almost all the way, the road follows close to the cliff edge, so for a change there were few hedges and ditches to slow our progress. As we climbed the hill of Knockmahon on the eastern side of Bunmahon Bay, a flock of grazing oystercatchers shared a field with a herd of Friesian cattle, making an amusing composition in black and white.

A short distance up the hill we came to a sturdy stone wall that once surrounded the ore yard, where ore waiting to be shipped to Swansea for smelting was stored. I took a brief detour down a little road beside this wall and found the little cove where tall-masted ships once were loaded from a long wooden jetty. There is a little modern pier there now, above which rich orange-coloured cliffs tower, streaked green in places, hinting at the copper ore that still lies within them.

Back on the road, we came across a sign warning us to beware of unprotected mineshafts, indicating that we had reached the business end of the Bunmahon mines, and a short distance farther on I climbed a fence into a field to throw a pebble down a gaping hole eight feet across, and listen for its fall. It was something I could remember doing as a child and being aghast at the time that elapsed before a hollow crashing sound was heard. This time, however, the wind was too strong and the beginnings of a shower of rain was spattering against my waterproof coat, drowning out the sound.

The stone wall lining the road was a mass of sea-pink cushions just coming into bloom, interspersed with violets and primroses. This stretch of coast as far as Kilmurrin Cove has the richest hedgerows for wild flowers that I know; unfortunately, it wasn't ordained that I should enjoy their fragrance on this visit, for rain came sweeping in waves off the sea. I groaned as I was forced to pull on my waterproof trousers, and stow away my map where it would not turn to papier-mâché pulp. Teresa continued on cheerfully, ignoring the grumbling of her companion. The fulmars also continued cheerfully with their mating aerobatics along the cliff edge, hovering in the strong wind and changing their wing shapes into an amazing variety of forms with absolute ease.

The ruins of a tall building loomed out of the rain inland from the road, with the legend 'BOCKERS RULE OKAY' adorning it in white letters two feet high. I think this was one of the engine houses erected in the 1820s which contained the lift machinery and the pumps for keeping the mine shaft clear of water. Back in use again in 1905 when the mines reopened briefly, this piece of industrial archaeology, and its attendant circular stone chimney perched on the high cliffs, represents the most dramatic visible remains of Bunmahon's mining past.

The cliffs along this stretch display frequent signs of collapse due to erosion. Tall slender columns of more resistant rock tower out of the sea, providing on their narrow summits, exclusive nesting for fulmars and kittiwakes, safe from all predators but the feathered kind. One such column here is noted on the ordnance map by the name Carrigada, or 'Long Rock', a descriptive if unimaginative title for a piece of rock that reaches up almost as high as the 170-foot cliffs.

At Kilmurrin Cove the sea eats deeply into the landmass to welcome a fast-flowing stream from the hinterland, the ancestor of which created the sweeping valley here as it drained the meltwaters of the Comeragh glaciers. The flat land on either side of the stream is strewn with great tussocks of grass, resembling herds of musk oxen.

On the eastern side of the cove as the cliffs rise up again, a long crevice can be seen where sometime in the distant past the roof over a deep sea cave collapsed. The cave that remains is named after St. Muirne, who is said to have founded a church nearby in ancient times; accessible only at very low tides, legend has it that the cave contains a miraculous statue of the saint. Canon Power, the Waterford antiquarian, managed to gain entrance 'with difficulty' in search of the mysterious statue, but all he found was a piece of stalagmite 'in which only a vivid imagination could detect a resemblance to the human form'. As we climbed the hill on the eastern side, we caught sight of Kilmurrin Cove's shyer inhabitants, a small herd of brown feral goats that graze the twilight zone between the sheer cliff face and the field boundaries.

Shortly after Kilmurrin Cove, the green headland of Dunabrattin, topped with its lonely World War II look-out post, could be seen stretching out into a rain-shrouded sea. The head is separated from the mainland by a substantial earthen fortification, making it one of the largest promontory forts on this coast. The name Dunabrattin is translated as Dun na mBreatan, or the Fort of the Britons, and I have heard it said that the earthworks, which include a fort within a fort that can be clearly seen on the west side, date from the time of Christ.

We left the road and crossed the fields towards the point of the head, on the way climbing over the defensive earthworks, today reduced to mere field boundaries. From the look-out post on the promontory, the view up and down the coast is said to be extensive, but all we saw was the indistinct blue-grey shape of cliffs extending east and west into the curtains of rain.

Dunabrattin Head provides protection for a small fishing harbour known as Boatstrand. It is not exactly a village, rather a gathering of pleasant cottages along the road above the simple sheltered pier. An upturned curragh, the traditional tarred canvas-hulled fishing boat of the west of Ireland, displayed its black curved keel in front of a thatched cottage near the pier, giving the place a Connemara air. In a field nearby stood a dilapidated old railway carriage that in its retirement must have housed many a happy holidaying family. We came to a little shop called Waterford Woodcraft, and the display lighting on the beautifully turned wooden plates and ornaments lured us inside. It was a relief to be out of the rain briefly, but I felt like the proverbial bull in a china shop, moving between the close-stacked shelves with a large knapsack on my back, so we were soon back in the wet again.

On the roadside above the harbour a horse-box lorry was parked, and a thoroughbred mare was being led down the hill to the little strand beside the pier. We stopped and got chatting to the driver and a companion who stood in the lorry sheltering from the rain.

'The horse is bein' swum', the driver said in answer to my naive query as to where the animal was being taken.

'What for?' I asked, half believing I was being taken for a ride and I would get a joke answer.

'In case they would get a skin problem or get a cut in a hunt, ye train 'em when they're young to do these things. If ye train 'em to swim when they're young, you've no problem when they're pushin' on.'

'So sea water is good for them?'

'Oh it tis to be sure, you've salt and iodine for free out there.'

'Is it not very cold to be putting the horse in the water?' Teresa asked.

'Not at all', he replied, smiling, 'there's no cold in that water, oh no.'

And sure enough, the man below with the horse walked along the pier leading the horse out the strand below him on a long rope until the animal was swimming. Round the pier she swam and regained her footing on the strand at the far side, before doing the return journey.

Leaving this touch of rural life behind, we left Boatstrand and headed up the coast towards Annestown. The road dropped down and swung inland to cross another stream at Knockane where the first trees we had seen since Bunmahon were growing in the garden of a pleasant seaside bungalow. Before long we were walking down a long straight road into the village of Annestown, reputed to be the only village in Ireland without a pub. It is probably the only village without a Catholic church as well, and I could not help wondering was there a connection!

Annestown appears to have begun life in the late eighteenth century when Henry St. George Cole, a relative of the then Earl of Enniskillen, was made agent for his Waterford holdings in the 1790s and settled here. After military service in the West and East Indies, Cole had commanded the Crown forces in County Cavan that had 'dealt' with the 'Hearts of Oak' movement, a secret society similar to the Whiteboys of the south-east. He was immediately welcomed to the area by the Waterford landlords, who were experiencing similar difficulties to their Cavan brethren, and before long was prominent in the prosecution of the Whiteboys and the terrorising of the Irish populace. During and after the '98 rising, together with Uniake of Woodhouse in Stradbally and Hubert May in Waterford, he ruled the county with the sword.

The houses of the village and a Protestant church are perched on the side of a hill along a road which drops steeply into a broad valley behind the beach. A sturdy sea-wall with an amphitheatre of rounded cobbles piled against it resists the attempts of the sea to inundate the valley. High tides cover the fine sandy beach, ensuring that it is always spotlessly clean.

A half-mile inland can be seen the Arthurian profile of the ruined Dunhill Castle, a le Poer fortress built on a tall crag of rock. When Cromwell swept across Waterford in 1649, one of his priorities was to deal with the powerful le Poers. Having looked after the Curraghmore branch twenty miles to the north, his army moved south to invest Dunhill Castle.

The castle at the time was occupied by the Countess of Dun-Isle, and she encouraged her retainers to put up a spirited resistance to the Roundheads. It is said that she possessed one powerful piece of ordnance which in the hands of her master gunner made things very difficult for the Cromwellians. This master gunner, unfortunately, had an insatiable appetite for strong drink, and required to be kept well-supplied throughout the battle. Eventually, as his aim began to suffer, his mistress claimed they had run out of the hard stuff, and offered him buttermilk. The man was so insulted that he refused to fire another shot, and the Countess had to surrender!

The ruins of Dunhill Castle are well worth a visit. The last time I was there, however, a huge dribbling bull was guarding the gate. Beside the gate were two signs, one saying 'Private Property' and the other 'Beware of Bull: Survivors will be Prosecuted'!

The bay at Annestown is sheltered to the east and the west by cliffs, crags and islands, and at low tide there are an abundance of rock pools teeming with a rich variety of fish and crabs; good hunting grounds for children with nets and buckets. When the tide comes flooding into the pools, providing timely salvation for the survivors, the beach is a great place from which to swim. The crystal clear waters, the rocks and the clean sandy bottom offer plenty to entertain the skin diver, from large flatfish and crabs to sea urchins and sometimes shoals of larger fish.

Illaunaglas or Green Island, the larger of the great rocks jutting out into the sea on the eastern side of the bay, has a dripping cathedral-like cave running under it from one side to the other. Behind the beach, set into sloping grassy banks, there is an old limekiln that in its retirement has provided countless hours of play for children over the years, in the guise of a battlemented castle to be defended heroically or stubbornly besieged.

A few days after Teresa and I made a rain-drenched entry into Annestown, I returned to the village to follow the coast to Tramore, in the company of Jim O'Callaghan. The weather had changed radically, and it looked like we would have blue skies and sunshine all the way. Before starting out we delayed for a while beside the stream that flows under the coast road and into the sea. It seems to have no official name in spite of being quite a respectable watercourse, and is known locally as 'the river'! Three young horses grazed the tight grass at the river's edge, making a marvellous rural scene against the backdrop of Dunhill Castle up the valley. The pool beneath the bridge was full of large mullet, and we watched mesmerised as they lazily circled each other, causing ripples and tinkling splashes in the otherwise mirror-like surface of the water.

We were greatly tempted to loiter in this peaceful place, to 'hold our hour and have another', but we eventually dragged ourselves away with the consolation of knowing there were more riches to come. Turning off the coast-road towards the cliffs, we passed a field in the centre of which stood a six-feet high *gallan* or pillar stone, around which were gathered a large herd of heifers. They suddenly scattered and ran downhill towards us at a considerable pace for animals of such size and apparent clumsiness, an impressive thundering stampede. After milling about at the bottom of the field for a few minutes, the herd, without warning, turned and galloped uphill again and gathered around the *gallan*, snorting and steaming. Before we had gone much farther towards the sea, they were going through the strange process again.

On our way up the cliffs, Jim and I came across the fosse and ditch of a promontory fort overlooking Green Island. We stomped about in the thick springy grass, looking for signs of the hut site my research indicated was there, but found no trace.

The cliffs along this section of coast, like others I had passed on my way from Youghal bridge, had been subject to constant erosion, and since I had been familiar with these particular ones from my childhood, it was clear to me how much land had disappeared into the sea in the past thirty years. Jim and I followed a pathway that in places seemed to have renewed itself further and further inland as great slices of rock and earth collapsing onto the shore below removed sections.

Not far east of Annestown, Jim and I spotted the first chough of the day, making its unmistakable whistle-like song as it jinked and dived along the wave-effect created by the cliffs. As usual on these cliffs, fulmars were never very far away, glorying in the same air currents. From the following paragraph I found in an 1858 tourist brochure entitled 'Guide to Tramore and Surrounding Scenery', it is a wonder any fauna survives here:

> . . . fowl are to be met in plenty, the shooting at which affords good sport. . . . Seagulls, cormorants, murs, hagdowns, gannets, puffins, sea parrots, mother carey's chickens, blackdivers and ticklaces; and inshore about the rocks and islands wild pigeons, sealarks, curley, maybirds and Cornish daws. Rabbits, seals and otters are occasionally met with; and when fish are in plenty, gurnet, goat and mackerel playing over the water can be shot at in great numbers.

Puffins and gannets are no longer to be found along these cliffs; the nearest colonies today are on the Saltee Islands, almost

91

thirty miles away. Mother Carey's chickens was the name current at the time for petrels, which have almost vanished from the area completely, and certainly do not nest here. Cornish daws are our choughs, once quite common, now an endangered species in Europe: seventy per cent of the choughs of the British Isles are to be found in Ireland.

Today, I am glad to say, one can walk the cliffs to Tramore without having to dodge gun-toting tourists shooting at everything that moves! It would not have been unusual at that time to find local people climbing down the cliffs to catch sea birds or take their eggs for food which, along with fish, formed a normal part of the coast-dweller's diet up to and into the twentieth century. On the English coast seabirds' eggs were commercially collected and sold: in 1884, 130,000 guillemots eggs were sold in the London markets, and as recently as 1935, 300,000 black-headed gulls' eggs were sold at market.

The fulmar, whose beautifully controlled cliff-edge flying I had admired all the way along the coast, was very rare in the last century throughout the British Isles except in the Scottish island of St. Kilda, where it formed a central part in the survival of the inhabitants. About 12,000 of the birds were killed there each year for their meat, their oil which was used for lamps, and their feathers which were used for bedding. Instead of becoming extinct, the species multiplied and spread south and west, and is now common on all coasts.

As we passed the 200-feet contour and were following a narrow pathway along the cliff edge, we came upon a pigeon perched calmly on a tuft of dried thrift beside the path. The bird made no move to fly away as we approached. It was not a rock pigeon, the sort that frequent sea cliffs and fly in small flocks, but a larger and more colourful bird. We took some bread from our knapsacks to feed it but the bird, although not afraid of us, just was not interested. A direct attempt by Jim to pick the bird up resulted in the pigeon taking flight momentarily over the precipice and settling again a few inches away, the glossy iridescence of its plumage gleaming and glittering in the sunlight. The movement drew our attention to coloured rings on one of his legs, and we decided it must be a racing pigeon taking a rest en route.

We set off again, leaving the athletic bird to its own devices, and when we looked back a few minutes later it was still perched placidly on the cliff edge.

To the west of Kilfarrasy Island, about a mile from Annestown, we came across a rough track in a cutting that sank down deeply through boulder clay leading to a stoney beach. We made our way down to the beach to investigate a floating object we could see moored to a crag just offshore, and crunched across the deep bank of pebbles to the water's edge. It turned out to be a large semi-submerged raft containing cages full of lobsters, being kept alive and fresh before delivery, probably to the restaurants of Paris and London.

The beach was made up of the most magnificently polished and rounded pebbles of quartz, jasper, sandstone, limestone and flint, deposited along the shore in colourful graded banks. I am sure that the unfrequented nature of the beach was the reason why particularly beautiful examples were so thick on the ground; I found it impossible to resist collecting some fine jaspers which weighed down my pockets for the rest of the day.

When we had come down to the beach, we had disturbed a hawk which was now squealing and circling above us. Looking around to see if we could spot the nest the hawk was obviously defending, we noticed that the cliff-face was spectacularly columnar in form, like a miniature Giant's Causeway. A cluster of hexagonal basaltic rocks, part of a string of ancient volcanic lava flows that can be followed from this coast to Arklow Head, rose out of the sand and stone twenty or thirty feet into the cliffs before losing their distinctive shape.

Twenty feet above beach level, overhung by the massive cliffs, we could see the opening to what appeared to be a tiny Fingal's Cave. Leaving our knapsacks, we scrambled up to the opening, and, to our delight, found it was the entrance to a grotto, connected by a short tunnel to the open sea. Since it was low tide, we were able to clamber down into the grotto, the walls and ceiling of which were constructed from the same hexagonal basalt we had seen on the outside. The floor of the cave must have been about the same level as the beach, but was of highly polished rock with deep pools scooped out of it. At the back of the cave were piled a heap of large, rounded boulders, which had been polishing the floor and themselves to a smooth, glossy finish for centuries. The quality of the light reflected from the surface of the sea outside was most unusual, and the whole place had a 'Blue Grotto' feel to it, or maybe I should say Pink Grotto, because much of the rock was covered in an unusual pink sea lichen, something that probably would not survive in direct sunlight.

A subsequent search of *Placenames of the Decies*, written early in the twentieth century by the historian Canon Power, and the most comprehensive Waterford placename index, failed to turn up a name for this small but unique natural phenomenon.

We retraced our steps, and climbing back to the clifftops, headed eastwards once more. The next strand we came to was Kilfarrasy. Its sandy and stoney shore was deserted but for an elderly man and his very large wife, sitting in deckchairs. Descending to the beach to have our lunch, we passed by the couple, and as we did, the lady's deckchair collapsed with a resounding, splintering crack, depositing her unceremoniously onto the sand. Her squeak of surprise turned to a screech of laughter at the ridiculous situation. Jim and I turned to assist her into an upright position, finding it difficult to keep straight faces, but through the roars of laughter she insisted on staying where she was, saying she was in the safest place and she could not fall any farther ! Her husband grinned, half-bemused, half-embarrassed, and thanked us for our offer of assistance. We could still hear her hoots of laughter at the far end of the beach, where we sat on the rocks to have our lunch.

A man riding bareback on a fine thoroughbred mare came down the beach and inscribed a perfect circle of hoofprints in the sand at the edge of the tide. Round and round they went, moving in unison, locked into that perfect circle. When we left the beach, climbing the steep grassy slope to the pathway, they were still there, circling far below.

Although the grotto we came across earlier was strangely nameless, most of the marvellous caves, arches and rock formations along this coast do have names. The stories behind such places as the 'Cliff of the Pigs' and the 'Strand of Larry-the-Goat' may be lost to time, but Carraig an Iolair or Rock of the Eagle certainly refers to the time not too long ago when golden eagles frequented these cliffs. The historian Charles Smith states in his *History of Waterford* (1745) that the golden eagle and the osprey could be found along the coast at that time.

Nearly three miles out of Annestown the pillars at Newtown Head, marking the western portal of Tramore Bay, came into view ahead. We sat for a while in the clifftop grass overlooking Oileann na gCaorach and Oileann na BhFranncach, two high stacks with broad grassy tops. *Caorach* means 'sheep', but even Canon Power was undecided whether na BhFranncach means 'Frenchmen' or 'rats'! Up to the beginning of the nineteenth century, these two islets formed a narrow neck of land extending out from the mainland, pierced by two tall tunnels at sea level.The tunnels eventually collapsed into the sea, creating the two stacks that can be seen today. The original promontory was apparently the site of a medieval or early Christian settlement, indicated by the remains, under the burden of grass, or beehive-type *clochans* of the sort that only survive elsewhere in Kerry, and an earthen enclosure separating them from the mainland.

The next beach we came across was Garrarus, another stoney beach down to which we were able to make our way without difficulty. A few family groups were picnicking on the strand, the

children playing in the rockpools and laughing in the waves of the rising tide. Crossing a road leading to the beach, we climbed back to the cliffs hoping that Newtown Head would look a little nearer, but if anything it looked farther away. It was becoming a little cold as evening was being hurried in by a few rain squalls we could see to the west, so we stepped up our pace.

Beyond Garrarus the remains of yet another promontory fort survive, Oilean a 'Choite, enclosed by a double embankment, and the possible site of a stone fort. Half-a-mile from Newtown Head we came across two great guano-covered rocks offshore, that must be home to nearly two hundred cormorants. In the midst of all the comings and goings of this busy terminal, I counted sixty or seventy of the birds perched on precarious ledges.

At long last the three white pillars at Newtown Head appeared to be getting closer, and the fourteen-foot tall figure of the nineteenth-century sailor on one of them, the Metal Man, became clearer. He points out to sea to warn shipping to beware of being caught in Tramore Bay when storms blow from the south.

In the days of sail, before the erection of these pillars, numerous ships that were unlucky enough to mistake the bay for the relative haven of Waterford Harbour ended up either stranded on the broad sands or being broken up on the rocky headlands that enclose the bay. The best-known victim of Tramore Bay was the military transport ship *Seahorse*, which was driven towards the shore by a fierce storm in January 1816. On board were 292 soldiers returning from overseas, together with 71 women and children. Tramore people watched helplessly from the shore as the vessel was pounded inexorably towards the rocks of Newtown Head. There she was smashed to pieces, only 30 of the 363 on board managing to make it to safety. It is said that since the disaster the phantom band of the *Seahorse* is heard from time to time playing an air called 'Reel na Daibhche' in the remote places at the end of Tramore Strand.

The *Seahorse* disaster was the worst of many, and eventually led to the tall pillars, two on Brownstown Head, and three on Newtown Head, being erected as warnings. Lloyds of London are said to have contributed the Metal Man, which has become to

Tramore what the Eiffel Tower is to Paris. In recent times Irish Lights, which has the responsibility for maintaining the pillars and the Man, have attempted to sell or give them away, because they are obsolete and expensive to maintain.

As Jim and I walked through a meadow towards Newtown Head, we came upon a hare crouching in the grass. We stopped within two feet of the animal which, caught completely by surprise, froze. It seemed to quiver all over as I opened my camera case very slowly, making no sudden movements. I was just anticipating the fine close-up I would get and starting to focus the lens when, like a flash, the hare bolted off at phenomenal speed and vanished into the hedge nearby.

If you hop on one leg three times around the pillar that the Metal Man stands upon, it is certain you will be married within the year. Jim and I were happy to avoid taking this test, so we did not delay at Newtown Head, but headed north east along a fine cliff path towards Tramore, now just over a mile away.

Newtown Cove is a sheltered wooded inlet, as popular among the elderly of Tramore as a place to enjoy the sun as it is amongst the younger and more able bodied who swim and dive in its deep waters. As we passed through it, even the small gathering of people there seemed to overcrowd the place, after the comparative solitude of our day. Joining and following the public road for the first time since Annestown, we came across an old-style gypsy caravan parked at a layby. A dark-skinned, long-haired young man was busy setting up camp for the night while a young woman prepared a cooking fire. As well as their pony, dogs and a goat, we could see a pet pigeon perched on the roof of the caravan.

We wished the travellers good evening, and, indicating their pigeon, asked about the one we had seen on the cliffs near Annestown.

'It was probably a racing pigeon you saw,' the man told us in a strong central European accent. 'The one we have here, we found on the roadside injured, probably hit by a motor. We cared for him, and after a while he recovered; he has stayed with us since. He is glad to be not racing all the time,' he smiled.

We chatted with these interesting people for a while. They told us they had come from the Continent and were touring the British Isles. Both seemed well educated, and were the nearest thing I have ever seen to the typical Romany gypsies of eastern Europe.

So onwards again towards Tramore, and passing by the road leading down to the little fishing harbour, we came to the Ritz Bar, a thatched place with tiny windows and a low door. We went inside to quench our thirst and celebrate our arrival in Tramore, and what a surprise we received; inside the Ritz is an extensive modern lounge bar with fancy lighting and enough hanging plants to shame the Amazon jungle. I thought of the public houses I had been in on my way from Youghal bridge, and compared their decor with this opulent drinking palace. Although the Ritz was colourful, bright and well ventilated, and the drinks were served efficiently, I think I prefer the darkness of Kirwin's Bar in Bunmahon, and the proprietors' curiosity in John Paul's of Mine Head.

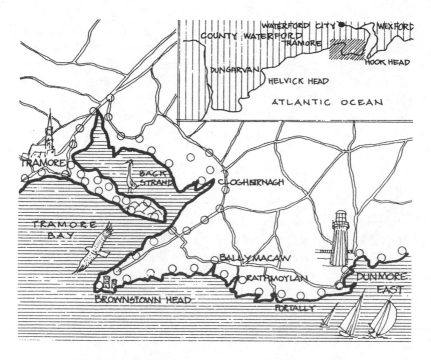

TRAMORE TO DUNMORE EAST

Tramore Bay is one of two great indentations in the coast of Waterford between the mouth of the Blackwater and Waterford Harbour, the other being Dungarvan Harbour. The two bights have many similarities, including extensive mudflats and long, narrow sand spits, but the beach at Tramore is not surpassed on the entire south coast.

Egan's *Waterford Guide* published at the end of the nineteenth century states:

> Our country wanting Tramore would be like an Indian god without the wonted diamond in his forehead – a rose without colour or perfume; a region of ancient and history fame, wanting the spot of modern colouring which enchants the superficial traveller and lures the society pilgrim in search of health and pleasure.

Egan was a Waterford city man, and every Waterford city man has a proprietorial interest in neighbouring Tramore. It is a kind of dual citizenship that is nurtured from an infancy spent playing on that long strand and in the thunderous waves, through adolescence, being thrilled by the rides, the garish colours and the loud music in the Amusements. The charm of Tramore appeals to all ages and all income groups, and has done so for two hundred years.

One of the earliest references to Tramore as a resort was made by the historian Charles Smith in his *History of Waterford* of 1746. For the next hundred years the growth of the resort was slow, and limited mainly to wealthy Waterford merchants who could afford to build elegant summerhouses there. Day trips from Waterford were popular, but to travel by coach to the sea often took nearly two hours. It was the construction of the railway between Waterford and Tramore in 1853 that opened the resort to the rest of the country and real tourism. Financed by the businessmen of the area, the seven-mile-long line was completed in a record time of 22 weeks at a cost of £5,500 a mile. Now the ordinary citizen of

Waterford could travel in style to Tramore in 25 minutes for as little as twopence, and the popularity of this new leisure activity, an outing by train, increased by leaps and bounds. The small railway carried nearly 75,000 passengers in 1862 and by 1867 this had risen to over 200,000.

During my childhood a major part of the fun of a day's outing to Tramore was the trip on the train, with the huffing and puffing of the old steam engine and the hum of happy children's conversation filling the smoky air. There was always a noisy queue at the station in Manor Street, and I can remember vividly the rush to get a good seat and the enthusiastic cheers when the locomotive slowly moved off, gaining speed gradually until the countryside seemed to be flashing by.

In the late 1950s the steam locomotives were retired and new diesel trains took over the route. While these machines were faster and cleaner than the old trains, they had few of the ingredients that made steam travel so thrilling. Anyway, the diesel did not last long; in the early 1960s the Tramore line became one of the casualties of government attempts to make national transport pay for itself. The line, like a number of other similar spur lines around the country, was not profitable, and as part of a national rationalisation scheme it was closed down. We now know that while the closure of many of our railway lines may have been a temporary economic necessity, the decision to sell off the land in thousands of parcels was short-sighted and disastrous. As fuel costs and the problems of high car ownership reach serious proportions, and lower cost electric-powered public transport systems become economically viable, the loss of all those lines will hurt even more.

When I was a child, Tramore was particularly festive for the August bank holiday weekend. Coaches and charabancs of all shapes, ages and colours brought crowds of day-trippers from places as far away as Counties Tipperary and Laois. The long, broad promenade became the stage for numerous side shows. I remember delicate-looking sword swallowers, tattooed escapologists festooned in chains, and even a fakir who lay on a bed of broken glass and had the fattest members of the audience stand on a plank on his chest. I can still smell the sweat and hear the strange English stage accents that most of these showmen had when announcing or dramatically explaining their acts.

In those days the back of the beach was lined with yellow and black striped bathing boxes where the older or more modest people changed into their swimsuits. My grandfather had a vast black swimsuit with shoulder straps, and I remember marvelling at how he could float, bobbing like a cork over the waves. The waves could be very exciting, but sometimes they became monstrous and exerted a dangerous undertow, and the lifeguards would raise the red warning flags on poles along the promenade.

The culmination of the day for many families was the picnic tea. Boiling water could be bought from residents of the house and cottages behind the promenade. You brought your own tea, milk and sugar, and a strong sweet brew was made to wash down prodigious numbers of egg sandwiches, banana sandwiches, and sticky buns. After tea it was time for the Amusements (what a wonderful term!) to be visited, a world of coloured lights, blaring music, bumper cars and slot machines.

My first flight in an aeroplane was from the beach in Tramore, where Captain Darby O'Kennedy thrilled hundreds each year flying them over Waterford in a twin-engined biplane. After queuing with my father for what seemed like ages, there was a rush to get on board, and I was swept up into the little cabin with a dozen others while he was left behind. This did not bother me at all, and I can vividly recall the unusual views that unfolded below as we passed over Waterford, expanses of slate grey roofs and dinky cars moving about amongst them. This same aircraft is still extant in flying condition, as Aer Lingus's mascot, taking the place of the first aircraft to fly scheduled flights for the company in the thirties – the Iolar.

I left Tramore on the next section of my walk to Waterford bridge on a dull grey July morning that seemed to promise rain. My aim for the day was to get as near as I could to Ballymacaw, a hamlet on the eastern side of Browntown Head, but my success or failure would depend on how easily I could cross Tramore's Back Strand. I started my circuit of Tramore Bay from the long promenade that lines the western side of the beach. The place was uncharacteristically deserted because it was not yet 9 am, and I set

off along the landward side of the thin peninsula that stretches two miles, to end in what is variously known locally as 'the sandhills' or 'the rabbit burrows', an impressive gathering of sand dunes covering over 200 acres, the tallest of which, Knockanriark, reaches almost 100 feet.

A full tide covered the Back Strand, and the gaunt triangular shapes that are all that is left of the old racecourse stand protruded from the glass-calm water. Seagulls line the top of the ruins, looking towards the Tramore Dump. It is hard to accept that there are no better possibilities for the location of such a virulent polluter of the environment than here within a hundred yards of a fine beach, draining into the Back Strand, which must be an ecologically endangered area.

Tramore has been a centre for organised horse-racing for centuries, and towards the end of the nineteenth-century the racecourse at the Back Strand was lauded as one of the finest courses in Europe. Originally the beautifully flat beach was marked out and used for races, but with the new railway bringing a great increase in spectators after 1853, a businessman called Delahunty established a permanent course at the back of the strand. Attempts had been made many times since 1820 to reclaim this tidal area; the original idea had been to block the Saleen, the tidal race between the sandhills and the mainland at Brownstown Head, but this proved too difficult. Subsequently, engineers succeeded in constructing effective dams across the Back Strand, providing sufficient land not only for the extensive racecourse, but for a golfcourse as well.

Roofed viewing stands with elegant cast iron columns were erected over the ensuing years, together with stabling for horses, dressing rooms and weigh-in rooms.

The shopkeepers of Tramore were not pleased with the location of the new racecourse, because many of the punters could get to and from the course without passing through the town, so when £5,000 was granted for the construction of a proper road to the course, they made sure it started in the town. This road, and the retaining wall to protect it from the sea, formed the basis for the present promenade.

Disaster struck the racecourse in 1911 when a winter storm, combined with a high tide, breached the dams. The following winter the sea burst in again. Gangs of men worked in the most dreadful conditions to carry out repairs, directed by the engineers involved in the construction of the new bridge at Waterford. Their efforts were in vain, however, and their work failed to withstand the elements. The racecourse gradually disappeared, tide by tide, until all that now remains are the stonework bases to the stands and the entrance facade to the saddle room. Even these will soon disappear under an ever-expanding tip-head.

The grass is tight and springy at the back of the rampart of stones that parallels the beach, and the perfume of the white clover in summertime is like a narcotic. The path leading to the sandhills was protected from the sea breezes and the constant roar of the surf by the rampart, and it was a very peaceful walk, with only the drone of bees and the calls of a large flock of curlews gathered at the edge of the still waters to intrude on the silence.

As I approached the sandhills, I came across the remains of one of the original dams, a wildflower-covered embankment stretching out across the Back Strand, its middle long ago washed away by the relentless tides. Among the first dunes, I passed a great heap of cockleshells and burnt stones, probably a kitchen midden left by the first inhabitants of the Tramore area. At the end of the nineteenth century the Waterford naturalist, R. J. Ussher, found in middens such as this the remains of flint instruments, pieces of red deer antlers and the bones of oxen, goats, horses, pigs and even those of the extinct great auk. Each time I pass this particular heap, I look carefully for some ancient stone artefact that has just been exposed by the wind for me to discover; I am not ambitious, a modest flint arrowhead would do, but I am afraid all I will ever see amongst the shells are shards of broken glass and Coke tins!

I mounted a sandbank between the midden and the sea, and walked down to the beach through clumps of sea holly surrounded by pink-flowered convolvulus. Suddenly I was in another world, with crashing waves and a stiff bracing breeze, the open Atlantic before me, hemmed in by Brownstown Head to the east, and Great Newtown Head, topped by the Metal Man to the west.

Tramore Strand is here covered with multicoloured pebbles from brilliant white quartz to blood-red jasper, and a surprising number of flint nodules. Strewn on this end of the beach I also found a wide and amusing array of flotsam and jetsam, from shoes of all varieties and styles, to a motorbike, complete except for its tyres and engine. A large, burnished and worn tree-trunk with twisted branches standing half-buried in the sand would not have seemed out of place in a gallery of modern art.

I came to the end of the peninsula about three-quarters of an hour after leaving the promenade. The tide was going out, draining the wide expanse of the Back Strand through the narrow outlet between the sandhills and the opposite shore, the Saleen. The strong current combined with a violent rip-tide to throw the surface of the sea into a frenzy, with waves going in all directions and crashing into each other.

Turning westwards again, I returned towards Tramore along the north coast of the sandhills, crossing marram-grassed ridges spotted with pink orchids and wild cabbage. Black and red burnet moths clustered on flowerheads and I constantly had to avoid stepping on slow-moving, bloody-nosed beetles crossing the track.

I could not resist clambering up the side of the tallest sandhill to see the view; Knockanriark must have lost at least some of its height over the years to trippers like myself scrambling up tracks like lava flows of sand through the marram grass. It is a tough if brief climb, but the reward is a great all-round view. A hundred feet below I could see cormorants and herons beginning to gather on the emerging sandbanks as the tide fell. Small flocks of terns darted above the receding water, and a kestrel, attempting to hover over an intended victim in the dunes below, was being mobbed by small birds and eventually had to give up and go elsewhere for its lunch.

I climbed down into the 'crater' of Knockanriark where the constantly shifting sand had exposed a scattering of beautiful pastel-shaded snail shells and the jawbones of some small mammal. A piece of an old clay pipe, some fragments of broken delph and what looked like chicken bones suggested the remains of a Victorian picnic had also been uncovered, or were the bones those of the great auk?

Amongst the tufts of marram grass along the dunes there grows a variety of ground-hugging blackberry which I have not seen elsewhere, bearing a rich dark purple berry with a bloom, superior in taste, in my opinion, to the hedge berry. The sheltered pathways through the central 'plains' of the sandhills were carpeted with the tiny flowers of wild thyme, and butterflies and grasshoppers scattered before me as I moved through the heady and aromatic air. This peninsula is a fascinating place, seeming utterly remote in spite of the nearness of Tramore, with a rich micro-ecology of its own. It is one of the few places I know in Waterford where owls can be seen frequently, birds which nest in the woods above the Saleen opposite, and cross the straits to hunt in the dunes here at evening time. Ireland's only true lizard, the Common Lizard, is plentiful here, as I know from the number of times our foraging children have been left holding the tails of those they caught while the owners escaped!

Here at night, in the middle of the dunes, the ghostly military band from the wrecked transport ship the *Seahorse* is said to have been heard. Another more exotic ghost is called Gormog or Garamooguh. He lives under the sea, and during the day comes no closer to the land than the third wave from shore. At night, however, he comes ashore on a white horse to tend to his livestock, a single small black cow which grazes on the thin salty grass. This cow is enchanted, having a purse in her left ear containing a magic shilling, which renews itself each time it is taken and spent.

When I got back along the beach of the Back Strand to the old embankment, it was clear that, although the tide was almost out, the depth and width of the breach in the dam was such that any attempt to cross this way to the mainland would be foolish. Instead I decided to try farther back at the tip-head, but I did not reckon on the small river that empties into the Back Strand from Riverstown. The river may have been small, but its apparent depth and the treacherous-looking mudbanks lining it soon put me off the idea. So I had to return almost to the point where I had started that morning, before I could usefully turn north. I made my way along the side of a wheatfield and through a local authority housing estate to Turkey Road, which brought me to the main Waterford road.

At noon, with about six miles covered, I crossed the sandstone bridge over the deep cutting in which the old railway once ran. I remember as a child being lifted up here to see the steam-train passing below through billows of smoke. Now the cutting contains a micro-habitat: a green swamp of reeds, willows and shrubs, a linear wilderness saved at least along this stretch from the despoliation of the developing seaside resort.

On the public road again, heading inland, it was a relief to have easier footing, even if the tarmac was harder on the soles of the feet. Bearing right off the main Waterford road beyond Riverstown, where the river I had failed to cross had become a bog, I walked uphill past an elaborate roadside shrine. Officially opened in March 1922 by Cathal Brugha, then Dail representative for Waterford, it was erected in memory of IRA men who had died during the War of Independence. A few months later Brugha himself was shot dead by Free State troops in Dublin's O'Connell Street. The names of those Waterford men who died on the Republican side during the subsequent Civil War were later added to the list commemorated.

When the public road turned inland again, I dropped down through the fields to the northern shore of the Back Strand. Near the shore I came across some red-bricked ruins which were probably associated with Kettlewells Lake, an inlet which was enclosed in 1899 and stocked with fish. It was advertised in the *Waterford News* in April of that year as Tramore Fishing Lake, and

a season ticket to fish there could be bought for one guinea.

From this point on the Back Strand, a very substantial embankment protecting large tracts of agricultural land from the sea, connects with the higher ground of the mainland. It was clearly the easiest route by which to follow the shoreline. Making my way along it, I passed a concrete pillbox built into it, a relic of World War II, now only keeping watch over the sea of broken bottles and plastic containers. In the midst of this scene of pollution, a family of herons, two adults and one young bird strolled looking for titbits in the pools. Farther out, a human family were collecting cockles, their voices as they called to one another ringing clear on the still air.

At the end of the embankment I continued along the shoreline towards Brownstown Head. When I drew level with the volcanic shape of Knockanriark rising out of the sandhills across the mudflats, I sat in the long grass by the shore to eat lunch. The weather had changed its mind and decided to put on a sunny day, keeping the showers for later, so I basked in sunshine as I ate.

When I moved off again, the going got quite rough along the shoreline, and I was forced to make my way into the fields where I had to cross hedges and fences every few minutes. A series of thick inpenetrable hedges eventually channelled me out onto the public road where I crossed over Bealanaslateen Bridge, which, before the lands to the south were reclaimed, crossed a sea inlet. Beyond this the Kilmacleague Pill empties into a long fiord-like sea inlet at Clohernach, and here I went out across the fields to see if I could find any trace of the church of St. Macleague, founded in the seventh century. Swallows quartered the meadow through which I walked, and I disturbed a heron that had been standing sentry, awaiting the return of the tide. The heron rose up majestically, folding his head onto his back and spreading his broad wings. He alighted on a treetop further on, making a magnificent silhouette against the sky, his beak a triangular medieval dagger, his neck serpent-like.

As I crossed the fields, I could hear, swelling and dying, the ghost-like voice of one of the funfair operators three miles away at Tramore, encouraging youngsters to terrify themselves on his tangle of hurtling steel.

Soon the profile of the sandhills was on the horizon again, with Brownstown Head reaching out into an azure sea. On a slight promontory, I found two fragments of ancient wall surrounded by grassy mounds and a scattering of gorse. There were the remains of the old church of Kilmacleague, or more accurately the remains of the last of a number of churches to be build here, since the promontory was chosen by St. Macleague as the site for small monastic settlement in the seventh century.The land surrounding the church, including the graveyard, was much disturbed in recent years, and the only evidence of what was before are aerial photographs taken some years ago by the Air Corps, which revealed a network of earthen banks and rectangular platforms around the church.

Only two fragments of the church walls remain, constructed from large stones, with a substantial batter on the seaward side. The depth of rubble within the building was such that a corbel which I presumed originally carried the roof truss, was only six feet off the ground. The ruins are near a forty-foot cliff which moves closer by erosion year by year. I'm told there was a graveyard here, and as the sea eroded the cliff of boulder clay, skeletons were exposed in a grisly manner until they fell into the waves below. It is difficult to imagine where the shoreline was when the church was in use, but it is clear that it must have been a dramatic setting.

The lands to the west of Kilmacleague have been reclaimed by the construction of a substantial embankment to hold back the sea, behind which, along a narrow lagoon, a line of herons stood spearing small fish. As I came to the edge of the cliff, I disturbed a flock of wimbrels on the shore below. They took off squealing angrily, and continued to circle and protest loudly until I left.

I returned inland along the banks of the Pill through an old-fashioned meadow, a pleasure to walk through compared to the heavy nitrogen-treated pastures elsewhere. Although the rich mixture of grasses and herbs reached my knees, they were as light as a feather to walk through, and as I disturbed them, they gave off a marvellous perfume. The seed heads of the grasses were dried in the summer sun, but six inches down in the sward the stalks were fresh and moist.

Crossing Kilmacleague Pill at Clohernach Bridge, I noticed what I at first took to be a thrush with a dark brown breast perching on a rock beside the stream. When I stopped to have a better look, the bird turned his back to me, a back that was an iridescent green-blue, and took off, his wings a blur of bright colour. It was a kingfisher, the first I can remember seeing along this coast. I walked on, looking off down the stream where he had vanished, and he suddenly returned at speed, flashing by me and under the bridge.

Not far from the bridge is a public house, and as I wearily approached it, I was set upon by a huge and fiercely barking St. Bernard, his great jowls dripping with thick saliva. Raising my stick (something that has never before failed at least to slow down barking dogs), I found that for once it had the opposite effect. Angered into an even greater frenzy with the temerity of this human to actually threaten him, he came at me all the more. Thinking with a speed that is only possible when sheer terror is the driving force, I looked about me for an escape route, and in a most undignified manner, I retreated in disarray, running as fast as I could for the pub door. The place was empty, dark and cool after the sunshine outside, and as I fell in the door a bald-headed man I took to be the landlord emerged from the back room.

'Do you own that dog?' I asked him, indicating outside, the fright I had got fuelling anger. The monster dog had not followed me in, but stood glowering just outside the door.

'No,' he said, 'We're just looking after it for someone.'

'Well it ought to be locked up,' I said, my anger rising at his nonchalance. 'Do you know it attacked me out there?'

'Ah, sure he wouldn't touch you, he's harmless,' he replied infuriatingly with a lazy smile.

As if to testify for him, the great woolly dog padded into the pub, and leaning on me licked my trouser leg, leaving a slimy trail of dog saliva.

'Well, it's one way to get customers,' I said as sarcastically as I could.

By this time I had covered twelve miles, and the heat of the day was beginning to get to me, so I decided to turn the situation to my advantage; I ordered a pint of beer. My brother Tom's house was a little more than a mile away at Corbally, out towards Brownstown Head, and I decided to end my day's walk there.

After a very refreshing pint, I was on my way again, up a hill and down into a deep hollow where another stream ran into the Back Strand, and where the local church nestles, a comparatively recent building of purple sandstone. Because the church is so secluded, its bell-tower is located on the hill above it, in the back garden of a new bungalow.

It was nearly three o'clock when I reached my brother's house, where, I spent a glorious hour luxuriating in a hot bath.

The stretch to Dunmore East was resumed a few days later. I was glad to have the company of Jim O'Callaghan again, who always finds a good country walk hard to resist. The sun was high in the sky when we set out, but there were only about seven miles to cover and we were in no hurry. As we walked downhill towards the shore at the Saleen, the wildflowers in the meadows around waved in a light breeze, wafting heady perfumes that blended with the salty smell of the sea. Ahead, the tide was receding from the Back Strand in turquoise and ultramarine stripes, and racing white-flecked through the narrow channel between the sandhills and Saleen.

Saleen Beach starts rather narrowly and meanly, but broadens out into a fine strand, backed by an expanse of wildflower-strewn sea-meadow. Its microecology is very similar to that of the Tramore sandhills opposite, to which it must have been originally joined. A sign at the carpark warns against bathing here, although one look at the tidal race should be enough to convince most people of the danger of such a venture. A couple of exotic and expensive-looking speed-boats were moored offshore near a ski-jump ramp; when the tide is in, the sheltered and calm lagoon of the Back Strand must make a perfect place for water-skiing.

A little distance along the beach, where a trickling rivulet flows over a grass and bramble-covered bank, someone has built a miniature Marian shrine with a six-inch statue of Our Lady of Lourdes mounted in a blue painted cave. My maps show no holy well here or where this stream rises, so its origin remains a mystery.

The constant roar of the breakers across on Tramore Strand and the continual piping of the terns flying up and down the narrow straits filled the air as we walked south-west along the beach, crunching across cockle, periwinkle and razor shells. The three white pillars of Newtown Head on the west side of Tramore Bay came into view as we walked, followed by the bulk of Brownstown Head, the bay's eastern portal.

Up until about twenty years ago, the southern end of the beach was an excellent spot for catching sea bass. You could be sure of catching these fish only thirty minutes before and after high tide. Fishing is something I do not aspire to, but I used to enjoy watching anglers here expertly taking these fish from the sea. They arrived half-an-hour before the high tide, and dug vigorously with spades at the rising water's edge, exposing and capturing long, thin garfish-like creatures. These fish apparently bury themselves in the sand to await high tide, and when the water approaches, wriggle their way to the surface. This was a most convenient arrangement for anglers, because the bass come close into shore to feed off the sand fish. Baiting their hooks with these unfortunate creatures, the anglers strode into the surf to cast their lines with long solid-looking rods.

For a while nothing would happen, then all of a sudden the bass would start to bite, and in a frenzy of hauling in fish and rebaiting the hook, an experienced angler could have half-a-dozen fine fish up on the sand before, just as suddenly as they came, the bass were gone again.

At the end of the beach, Jim and I climbed up the rocks into the fields, the panoramic view of the bay evidence that we were now moving out to Brownstown Head itself. Walking alongside an earthen ditch that followed the cliffs, we suddenly heard the screeching of a hawk and had little warning before an angry kestrel dove on us like a Stuka. It came so low I clearly saw the bird's extended legs spasm as it emptied its bowels before pulling up into a climb, its 'cluster bomb' only missing us by inches because of the strong breeze along the cliff-edge!

Now two birds were circling us screeching Kee-kee-kee-kee, one, probably the female, coming quite close, the male circling at a distance as if a little embarrassed at his mate's behaviour, and reluctant to get involved. Realising that we must have happened upon their nest, we examined the cliff-face for some time without spotting it.

We were giving up when Jim sighted, on a projecting spur of rock about six feet below the cliff-top, what appeared to be a bundle of twigs. Perched in the midst of the twigs we could just make out the highly camouflaged form of a bird standing upright and perfectly still. Perfectly still that is except for its beak, which was most animated, for it too was kee-keeing at us!

We left the kestrel family in peace and were soon approaching the tip of the headland and the two circular pillars made from sandstone blocks that had been constructed here in 1822. The previous year when the government surveyors were carrying out preliminary work in the neighbourhood, they observed some unusual goings-on. On the basis of 'information received', the Revenue Inspectors stopped three carts carrying potatoes at Kilmacleague, and found under the potatoes a number of bales of tobacco. There followed a search of the entire Brownstown Head area, during the course of which a smugglers' hoard of fifty further bales of tobacco and a large volume of rum was found in caves at the end of the Saleen.

We sat for a while at the outermost point of the headland, soaking up the sun and admiring the view, which at once took in the rugged sandstone Coolum cliffs eastwards to Swine's Head, and the coast stretching westwards from the far side of Tramore Bay as far as Mine Head. Keeping the old pillars company on the tip of Brownstown is yet another watch post from the Emergency, of the same type I had already come across on Rams Head and Dunabrattin Head. My father, who was in the Local Security Force and later the Local Defence Force during the war, may have spent nights on guard here waiting for an invasion and wondering would it be the Germans or the British, or at one stage the Americans. He knew full well, with the meagre equipment they had available, they would stand little chance against modern

114

mechanised forces with air support. There was not a man in his company, he told me, that would not have given his all anyway, if there was an invasion.

As we headed eastwards we followed the edges of the fields between gently waving wheat or barley and the protective earthen bank along the clifftop, sometimes carefully crafted from turves of red clay and covered with thick bouncy tufts of sea grass. We had to swing inland slightly to cross a small stream trickling down the hundred feet to the sea at an inlet called Cloonliamgowel, which roughly translates as the 'Harbour of William the Foreigner'. Who William was seems to be lost in the past.

In the late eighteenth century, an incident similar to the case of the *Marie Deare* occurred between Brownstown Head and Ballymacaw. During a stormy spell of weather on a January evening, a small fishing vessel was returning to Dunmore when the men on board spotted a cargo vessel in some difficulty near

the rocks. When they went to the vessels' aid, they saw no-one on deck, and after hailing her for some time, they boarded. There was indeed not a soul on the ship, which they found to be Swedish and carrying a full cargo of hemp and iron. Nothing appeared to be disturbed on board, and the logbook's last entry was only a few hours before. Puzzled by the mystery, the fishermen got the craft under way, and sailed her up to Waterford to claim her as salvage. Within hours of their arrival at the port, a group of miserable seamen with not a word of English among them trudged into town, having walked by a circuitous route from Brownstown. They were the hapless crew of the Swedish ship, and when an interpreter was found they were able to tell their story. Terrified by the storm, they were convinced they were going to be dashed on the rocks at Brownstown, and so abandoned ship. Their lifeboat had been wrecked on the rocks under the headland and so they were unable to return to their vessel when the storm had eased off. They had no choice but to turn inland to seek help, and it had taken them almost twenty-four hours to find Waterford, and their vessel tied up safely at the quay!

The many wrecks on this coast have left a legacy of names associated with particular rocks or caves close to where the unfortunate ships succumbed, such as the 'Flour Hole', 'Palm Oil Hole', and the 'Swede Patch'. As time goes on however, the old local names are becoming lost for all time, because they were rarely written down.

Shortly before we reached the next inlet, a flash of unfamiliar colour caught our attention as a bright red fox crossed the field in front of us. He saw us and immediately headed for cover, moving inland rather than be hemmed in against the cliffs. He was careful to keep higher ground between himself and ourselves, and so we only glimpsed him once or twice before he disappeared. A few minutes later we were descending towards the cove of Ballymacaw.

Ballymacaw is a scattered hamlet of cottages and a few small pubs clustered about the inshore end of a deep ravine. We descended the fields towards the small beach, hoping to be able to cross to the cliffs on the far side without detouring too far inland.

After searching in vain for a passage through the thick thorn bushes that followed the steep sides of the ravine, we eventually found ourselves being diverted further and further inland. Crossing a seemingly innocent loose barbed wire fence, I found out too late that it was electrified, and received a mighty shock that felt like being kicked in the chest. I have had shocks from fences before, but never like this; I suppose the thickness of the barbed wire must have have something to do with it.

It was little consolation that the tree and bush-filled ravine we were trying to break through is nationally known among ornithologists as a location where rare migrant birds such as ring ouzels and pied flycatchers can be seen in season.

Ballymacaw would also be known in the world of ornithology for another reason. It is here that the last recorded great auk in the British Isles was seen in 1834; a few years later the bird was extinct. The great auk was a penguin-like bird about the size of a goose, and was very plentiful in the North Atlantic up to two centuries ago. Although a powerful swimmer like its cousin of the southern hemisphere, the penguin, it was a very slow mover on land, and suffered severely from predators during the laying season. So great was the slaughter of the bird by man during the late eighteenth century, it was declared one of history's first 'protected species' in 1794, but by then it was already too late. The great auk, Dodo-like, diminished steadily in numbers over the succeeding years, and by the time one was rescued from the sea in an exhausted state by a Ballymacaw fisherman in 1834, the species was extremely rare. The fisherman brought the bird home out of curiosity, and it survived a few months more on a diet of potatoes and fish. After it died, it was stuffed and mounted and is still preserved in Trinity College, Dublin.

About half-a-mile inland, Jim and I climbed a gate onto the public road, opposite a whitewashed public house. Capable at that stage of resisting anything but temptation, and since it was lunch time anyway, we entered the dark cool place, sparingly decorated, and ordered two pints of beer. We drank them outside, sitting on a garden seat in the sun and reviving our energy with sandwiches.

Refreshed, we resumed our journey, walking downhill

towards the sea, this time on the east side of the ravine. A terrace of by now familiar coastguard cottages lined the road, and near the beach their boathouse, built from sandstone with sharp limestone quoins, stood beside the road, sadly overgrown and with a collapsing roof.

On the road we came across a perfect specimen of what had been a silky black-coated mink, perfect that is except that it was completely flattened! Passing cars had done a neat job of removing the innards, leaving the pelt as new.

Ballymacaw beach is more than a hundred yards wide at the back of a deep sea inlet in which the hamlet's small salmon fishing fleet lay in sheltered moorings. The margins of the beach under the cliffs here are rich hunting grounds for shrimpers when the tide is out. A good path led up the eastern side of the cove out towards the cliffs, and in direct contrast to the far side, the landowner has made imaginative gaps and stiles in his fences to facilitate anglers who need to gain access to the flat rocks below the cliffs. While most of the fences and hedges I had encountered in the hundred miles I had travelled had posed little difficulty, it was certainly a luxury to use well built stiles. Out along the cliffs the path wended its way through masses of sea pinks and banks of white daisies, passing two secluded coves, flanked by high walls of pink layered Old Sandstone.

A familiar Kiough-kiough-kiough sound announced the presence of choughs, three of which we saw grazing in the field ahead of us before they took off. In the middle of this field we found a seven-foot sandstone *gallan*; at first sight it seemed to be cruciform in shape, but on closer examination I was disappointed to find that its shape had been caused by natural fault lines. Nearby on the clifftop we found a small timber cross inscribed with the sad message '1987, 13 years, in memory of Paddy Power'. Some young lad must have lost his life offshore here, as many fishermen have over the years. Not far from where we stood, a broad plateau of sandstone a few hundred yards offshore, called the Falskirt Rocks, has taken many fishermen. At high tide this field of rock is almost completely covered by water, and while the habitat it provides attracts a rich mixture of fish, lobsters and crabs, the sea protects its own by sweeping treacherous waves

across the rock that would upturn any small craft.

Twenty minutes after leaving Ballymacaw, we were dropping down a gently sloping field toward the next cove along this coast, Rathmoylan. In the 1920s and 1930s families flocked to little places like this for their summer holidays. They were usually not attracted by the glitter of a Tramore and probably could not afford it anyway, but preferred to fish, swim, and generally potter about. Their accommodation in little quiet places like Rathmoylan consisted of everything from a few large packing cases cobbled together to make a two-roomed *bothan*, to disused vans, buses and, for the elite, railway carriages. Into these cramped and not entirely weatherproof spaces families happily squeezed themselves, and had thoroughly uncomplicated holidays.

Rathmoylan still retains an ambience of holidays of old; a little Nissen hut that must have been there since the last war, a roly-poly caravan that could have antique value, and the little huts that have grown over the years, not so much in size as in solidity and respectability, all of them surrounded by neat postage stamp gardens.

Inland from Rathmoylan cove, on a prominence overgrown with young trees, thick brambles and elders, lie the remains of the old Rathmoylan church, abandoned since the nineteenth century. Until it was recently cleared, the graveyard surrounding it was a marvellously spooky place with eighteenth-century gravestones protruding through the ivy-clad ground under a green leafy canopy. Up to the mid-1970s there were a series of circular and rectangular earthworks in the field beside the church, which some intrepid historian said were the remains of the palace of O'Felan, prince of the territory, which in ancient times took in most of the county of Waterford. Whatever they were, the truth will probably never be known, because the field was subsequently levelled and ploughed.

We left the old-world atmosphere of Rathmoylan cove behind and, crossing the stream that runs onto the beach, ascended the east side of the cove, quenching our thirst with juicy blackberries from beside the path. A blackcap protested to us shrilly from the top of a bramble bush; he was a beauty, puffing out his pinky brown breast and throwing his all into his warning song. Out on the wild thyme fragrant cliffs again, we walked along the inland side of a beautifully and cleverly built wall of earthen sods, eroded into an almost natural bank. In places the sea had taken away great slabs of cliffs, exposing sheer precipices dropping vertically to the sea. Sand martins, whose burrows were visible in the clay just below the clifftop, whizzed up and down the path, hoovering up insects.

We passed through barley fields with margins thick with betony, and as we came to Swine's Head, Old Ship Rock came into view, looking like an old galleon with a high stern castle at anchor close to the cliffs. Inshore of the Falskirt Rocks, two fishermen had moored their lobster boat. They carried out their work in an unhurried manner, hauling lobsterpots on board and stacking them in the bow of the boat.

The cliffs now began to take on a most unstable look, as if some time in the not so distant past there had been a great subterranean disturbance. The clifftop was criscrossed with deep chasms, the bottom of which we could not see, and a massive skyscraper of rock had pulled away from the mainland and tilted seaward precariously like a pink Tower of Pisa. Some of the chasms were dangerously disguised by tufts of grass and gorse, and in one of them we were surprised to find two wrecked cars! The place made us feel decidedly uncomfortable; there was a geological fragility about it, as if anything could happen at any moment. We moved inland towards the safety of the barley field, on the way to which I nearly went feet first down a horrific hole. It was a relief to reach the field edge.

The coast of Wexford had been visible on the eastern horizon for some time, and it was now close enough to make out individual houses scattered along the shore. Black and white striped Hook Tower stands at the southern extremity of the coast, a lighthouse that always look nearer than it actually is, because of its great size. It is variously said to have been built by Raymond le Gros, Strongbow's right hand-man, Ross McCrew, the founder of the town of New Ross, and another Norman who came to Ireland with Henry II, Florence de la Hogue. Whoever built it, they did a remarkably good job; there are few places along this coast more exposed than the Hook peninsula. The lighthouse you see today

is simply a modern 'top' put a hundred feet up on an original stone tower that has certainly weathered more than five hundred winters.

The pathway we walked became more worn as we began to descend a hillside, covered with heather interspersed with dog-roses, into the next cove – Portally. As we walked along the rocky flanks of the cove, I heard kittiwakes calling as they wheeled above us, proof indeed that we were coming close to Dunmore East, where there is a large colony of birds.

What a beautiful place Portally is in the summertime with its thyme and heather-clad cliffs enclosing a narrow blue-green bay. In certain light conditions the cove could be mistaken for one of the renowned bays at Paleokastritsa in Corfu.

The Mediterranean ambience of the place was further strengthened while we sat on the rocks above the beach; a large speedboat came around the cliffs, the roar of its engine reverberating off the walls of the cove. As it nosed into the beach, the engine was cut, and a party of three men and a woman jumped onto the stoney beach. Within minutes, they had chairs and a table set up, and were unpacking a sumptuous picnic.

We left them to it, and as we ascended the cliffs again Portally cove was ringing with conversation and laughter.

An extensive slab of rock just offshore looked snow-covered with the guano of the many generations of cormorants and shags that have nested there. These birds are certainly hardy; inland species would not last long in winter conditions around these coasts. I find it particularly fascinating that seabird young seem to thrive on exposed and bare rocks that, although above high tide level, must be constantly showered by waves during storms. Some seabirds like guillemots and razorbills lay their eggs on the bare rock surface without a nest; their eggs are pear-shaped to prevent them from rolling off the ledge on which they are layed.

A good pathway along the cliffs between Portally and Dunmore took us up high above the sea again on red-pink old red sandstone cliffs that are eroding dangerously in places. I suppose they are entitled to have a little erosion now and then; they have been here for four hundred million years and are amongst the oldest sea cliffs on the south coast. The path followed the margin between the cliff edge and the cultivated land, a kind of linear meadow which widens and narrows according to gradient and erosion. This separate zone was rich in colourful wild flowers all the way along, attended by bumblebees, butterflies and burnet moths.

Bishop's Cave is a landmark nearer Dunmore, a great hole in the ground three hundred yards inland from the cliffs, connected to the sea by way of a cave. The cave can be entered by boat, and at one time it was a spectacular blow-hole, but we found it too full of redundant washing machines and old crashed cars to give a reasonable performance today. Not far from here we met a girl with a camera slung around her neck coming along the path from Dunmore. It occurred to me that she was the first person I had come across since I had left Youghal bridge who was actually walking the coast for pleasure!

As we neared Dunmore, we that found the great shelves of sandstone that extend into the sea from the base of the cliffs were occupied by a number of anglers, casting spinners far into the rising tide with long mast-like rods, and even as we watched, some were pulling in mackerel.

On Red Head, at 147 feet above sea level the highest point along this stretch of coast, I really felt that I was leaving the open sea and entering Waterford Harbour; the 180 degrees of Atlantic horizon I had had for much of the journey from Youghal bridge was now reduced dramatically. With the town of Duncannon on the Wexford side of the harbour now clearly in view, we began to descend towards the radio station perched on the promontory above the harbour at Dunmore. The path dropped down as the cliffs were interrupted at a place called the Flat Rocks — what remains of the quarry where much of the stone used to build Dunmore harbour was taken from in the early nineteenth century.

As we reached the village of Dunmore East, my walk from Youghal bridge had topped the hundred-mile mark.

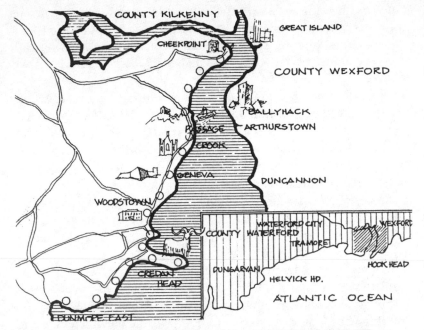

DUNMORE EAST TO CHEEKPOINT

The first time I holidayed in Dunmore as a child, we stayed in a converted bus perched in the grass above the Flat Rocks. When the weather was good, we had the finest view in Dunmore, while in stormy weather we could experience the full fury of the wind and sea in relative comfort; the rocking of the old bus adding to the excitement as the spume from vast waves bursting on the rocks below lashed against the windows.

The history of Dunmore East is vague until the mid-eighteenth century; the earliest physical evidence of human habitation in these parts was probably the Dun Mhor, or Great Fort, which occupied the clifftop above the harbour, and originally enclosed an area of more than one and-a-half acres. I say was, because half the great embankments and ditches that surrounded the enclosure were demolished in the eighteenth century when the harbour was being constructed, and the rest were bulldozed during the 'improvements' to the harbour carried out in the early 1960s.

The Office of Public Works, the government branch that looks after our ancient monuments, also has responsibility for harbour construction, and it seems that it was under their supervision that this vandalism took place.

The remains of a stone-built circular tower at the other end of the village suggest that the Normans took a liking to the place for a while, and in 1297 Dunmore was in the ownership of a Michael le Flemyng. Little is recorded between this and the mid-seventeenth century when a population of five was noted. A century later a Henry Mahon was reported as occupying an 'agreeable seat' called Nymph Hall situated slightly to the north of the Strand Hotel in Lower Dunmore. At that time it is probable that there was a small community of fisherfolk living in *bothans* close to Counsellor's and Lawlor's Strands where they could launch and draw up their boats.

It took the establishment of the Mail Packet Station in Dunmore to put the place properly on the map. Because tidal and navigational difficulties in the Suir tended to slow down shipping between the coast and Waterford City, mail boats in the early nineteenth century to and from England used Passage East as a base. From here the mail would be transferred by dispatch rider or fast coach to the city. However, even Passage had its problems with sandbanks, tides and contrary winds, so a survey of Waterford Harbour was carried out to select a better location for the Mail Station. Dunmore East was identified by the Scottish engineer Alexander Nimmo as being a suitable location. With the assistance of Lord Waterford and Earl Fortescue, who both owned land in the district, Westminster was successfully lobbied to authorise the change and vote the necessary funds for the construction of a harbour.

Nimmo was commissioned to design the new harbour, and he chose for its site a little bay surrounded by cliffs called Portcallin. Work began in 1815, and a substantial pier was constructed between the mainland and a little stoney island called Oilean na gCloch, providing a wide and deep protected basin for the packet boat.

In obtaining the material for the pier part of the Great Fort was destroyed, before a rail connection was made to the Flat Rocks, where the bulk of the rest of the stone was quarried, cut and prepared. A particularly nice and unusual touch in Nimmo's design was the inclusion of the lighthouse as a finely proportioned Doric column, not as dominant today in the much expanded harbour, but still in perfect condition and performing its original task.

The first King's harbourmaster to be appointed to the new mail station was a County Waterford man named Mark Anthony, from Stradbally. He had joined the English navy as a midshipman in 1805 and his introduction to battle was against pirates off Cuba, where in true swashbuckling style he was involved in hand-to-hand fighting while boarding pirate vessels. He also took part in the Battle of Trafalgar on board *H.M.S. Naiad*, and was wounded by enemy gunfire in skirmishes in the Baltic. After this exciting career, with a limp and scars that must have impressed the little boys of Dunmore, he took up his post in 1823. Within nine years it was decided that a larger vessel was needed, and since the harbour at Dunmore was small and was giving some unforeseen problems of silting up, the mail boat ceased to call there.

The pier remained almost unchanged until the early 1960s, when major work to expand the haven and its facilities provided the improvements necessary to bring fishing in the area into the twentieth century. Unfortunately, the best of the picturesque qualities of the harbour disappeared in the improvements.

Back in 1825, when the new harbour was completed, the population of Dunmore increased dramatically. Lord Waterford built a large hotel above the harbour, and cottages were erected along the new coach road to Waterford for those employed in the Packet Station. For a number of years there were two villages — the original fishing village in Lower Dunmore, and the 'new community near the Harbour — but the beauty of the place soon attracted the wealthy of Waterford, particularly Protestant and Quaker merchants, to build their summerhouses on the cliffs facing the broad expanse of the harbour. I can remember as a child the term 'Little Belfast' being benignly ascribed to the village because of its Protestant majority.

The Fishermens Hall is Dunmore East's community centre and library, and has provided a home for public meetings, dances, plays, and films for well over a hundred years. My favourite memory of the place is when it was used as a cinema by a travelling movie man in the fifties and early sixties. The entertainment provided by the film being shown was secondary to that offered by the young cinemagoers, who cheered and jeered the actors and joined in the action. I clearly remember one night everyone taking part in an hilarious pillow fight that left the Hall covered in feathers. Such niceties as 'lip-synch' were not thought important by the stoic master of ceremonies, and part of the fun was trying to guess which on-screen character was actually speaking!

Further on, beyond a short street of cosy thatched cottages, Dunmore East's park divides the road from the sea, its well-kept lawns sloping down to a couple of beautiful rocky coves. The large cedars in the park are reputed to have been planted by King George V, during a visit as a young man to a lady friend in the village.

The flamboyant facade of the Haven Hotel overlooks the park. Built around 1850 by David Malcolmson of the Waterford shipbuilding family, it was inspired, it is said, by the chateaux that he and his wife saw on a holiday in France. It was designed by John Skipton Mulvany, whose other works still surviving include

Broadstone Railway Station in Dublin and Athlone Railway Station. Malcolmson's son Joseph was not interested in the family business, and only wanted to go to sea as a fisherman. He died young, however, and the Fishermens Hall, originally called Malcolmson Hall, was built by his mother in his memory.

Turning to the right beyond the Haven Hotel, the road drops steeply and winds down to Lower Dunmore. Nearby are the remains of Dunmore's oldest built structure, a round Norman tower, probably part of what was a large complex of buildings. Next to this an Englishman named Jacob had a small bakery in the last century, making 'dog biscuits' for the fishing fleet. He eventually moved to Dublin, where it is said he adapted the dog biscuit, developing the creamcracker, which helped to make Jacob's Biscuits the big name they are today.

Lower Dunmore is dominated by the Strand Hotel, which overlooks the beach atop a high stormwall, constructed like the harbour from great blocks of local sandstone. I feel privileged to have known this place in what now seems to be another age. When I was a child holidaying in Dunmore, the Strand Hotel was called Lawlor's Hotel, run by the tall thin bespectacled Mr Willie Lawlor. An ancient handpowered petrol pump stood in the forecourt, and the front ground floor was devoted to a bar on the left, connected by a door to a general grocery on the right. No part of the hotel seemed to be out of bounds to children, guests or not; indeed they seemed to be encouraged to wander around. A visit to the kitchen at any time of the day or night would provide a generous sandwich of freshly sliced ham or a piece of cake and a glass of milk.

A couple of days after I had reached Dunmore with Jim O'Callaghan, I set out again on my own, heading upriver towards Waterford, now less than twenty-five miles away. It was low tide when I walked through Lower Dunmore, so I was able to cross to Counsellor's Strand along the rocky shore. It is a lovely place to swim from, and very safe for young children, who when they are tired of swimming and making sand castles can explore the flat slabs of sandstone that extend out from cliffs called Cathedral Rocks. Just around the corner from the beach is a marvellous cave, where for nearly two hundred years people who passed by have carved their names. The earlier autographs are beautifully engraved in fine Roman and italic lettering, the later ones using more utilitarian styles that took less time. 'RC BUTCHER 1839' seems likely to spend many more years in the company of P.A. POPE and J.A. SWAN, and S. Going, who was aged 10 when he or she left a neatly carved signature in 1959. The most poignant inscription says:

> Each Persons as you here pass by
> I hope you not me name dead
> W Butle 1866

I had walked the cliffs eastward from Dunmore many times, and I looked forward to renewing my acquaintance with them as part of my walk from the Blackwater. It is along this stretch at Credan Head, that the Waterford coast finally relinquishes its

connection with the open sea, and becomes increasingly a river bank.

Remembering the steep muddy track that years ago was the only access to Counsellor's Strand, I climbed the neat tarmac path up to the carpark behind the beach, and continued up towards Foilakipeen Hill. Great white trumpets of convolvulus adorned the hedges, and the air was filled with the scent of woodbine. Perched on top of the hill are two tiny timber huts painted a lively blue, surrounded by a confusion of wallflowers, with one miniature door and window in each, two more marvellous examples of what holidaymakers used to live in when they came to the seaside years ago.

I went through a gateway beside them, and crossed a field sloping down towards the cliffs. The Saltee Islands came into view to the east over the Hook peninsula, just behind Loftus Hall, an unmistakable grey fenestrated slab standing in an almost bare landscape. Originally called Redmond Hall after the family that owned it and the surrounding lands, it came into the ownership of H. Loftus after the Cromwellian Wars. His descendants went steadily up in the world, became Viscounts and eventually the Marquesses of Ely. Through most of this century Loftus Hall was a Convent, but in recent years it was bought from the nuns and converted into a hotel.

The field I walked through along the edge of Waterford harbour was stocked with a fine healthy herd of Friesians, and rabbits which had been grazing amongst them, darted away at my approach. There is no defined cliff path on this side of Dunmore, and one has to cross hedges frequently, heading inland every so often to ford little streams. Meadow pipits rose continually before me, incessantly singing their mild disapproval of my presence. There is an abundance of wildlife along these cliffs, each time I passed close to a blackberry bush I could hear a rustling scurry as some unidentified mammal, caught off guard by my approach, made his panic-stricken escape. The low cliffs are richly clad and thick with gorse and hawthorn, making it an excellent wildlife habitat.

The sun came out as I followed tractor tracks through fields of ripening barley, bathing Slieve Coillte and Kennedy Park across the harbour in a brilliant light. Ahead, the grey slated roof of Credan Cottage, one of the few farmhouses along this stretch of coast, came into view, sheltered by a bower of cypress trees. Passing a huge shrub of purple-flowered wild mint, laden down with insects, beetles and moths, I left the fields and walked down a track leading to the house. A neatly kept sandstone-built cottage with an almost continental flavour, it has, like many farmsteads of the nineteenth century and earlier, a gable belfry.

Skirting the cottage, I passed along the edge of a barley field and soon a new view of the Wexford side, taking in the town of Duncannon, came into sight. Bearing around towards the east as I followed Credan Head out into Waterford harbour, I spotted a movement on the cliff edge, and found myself looking at a herd of woolly, brown and white wild goats. There were about eight of them, grazing the narrow strip between the barbed-wire boundary of the field and the sheer red sandstone cliffs. When I approached, they quickly made themselves scarce, following a long-horned ram down cliff paths and out of sight. I was surprised that there was no sign that they ever had 'trespassed' into the field through the ineffective fence, to have a go at the thicker grass there. Their own territory was very sparse and rocky, and I wondered how they survived.

As I walked on, I could see that inland the sky was dull and black, looking very much like rain, while the coast was clear and blue-skied. This is a phenomenon particular to the area; somehow this south-east coastal edge of Waterford often seems to have a microclimate that keeps its sky clear when it is dull and rainy inland.

The highest point of Credan provides a unique 360 degree viewpoint of Waterford Harbour. To the south Dunmore and the open Atlantic can be seen, while to the north thickly wooded Knockaveelish guards Fornaght Strand, with the great white sweep of Woodstown beyond. To the west are hilly pastures, and to the east the Wexford coast shows off its eleven fine sandy beaches. Beyond the highest point, the terrain drops down very steeply into the sea, only a strip of thick gorse dividing the fields from the cliffs. I searched for a way down through the gorse to the 'Forty Steps', a landing place carved in the sandstone cliffs a century or more ago, that as children we were told was the beginning of a smugglers' route inland. Their real purpose was to give swift access to a boat in the days when pilots competed for the job of taking a ship up to New Ross or Waterford.

I have been down the steps many times, but on this occasion I found the gorse and brambles thick and vicious, and after fighting my way through them for a few yards with little sign of getting anywhere, I gave up and retreated.

I now turned westwards again and inland along the north side of the headland, where I found an area with some huge field mushrooms, the largest of which measured nine inches across. Passing through a gap in the high gorse bushes, I came across two little black and white puppies, wrestling and playing with one another. As I appeared, they barked at me and dived for the cover of a thick bramble bush, disappearing into a burrow through the thorns, and growling threateningly from its depths. I wondered if they were wild; the burrow in the bush looked very much like a den or a set.

Further on, I came to a boreen heading westwards, which I knew would take me to the public road just above Fornaght Strand. Originally the width of an ass-cart, the passage was narrowed by gorse, sloes and nettles overladen with garlands of perfumed honeysuckle, and I barely had room to pass. When I was young I was told this boreen was part of Bothar na mBan Gorm, a smugglers' route inland used in the sixteenth and seventeenth centuries. The story goes that the local inhabitants were warned by the smugglers to stay indoors on certain nights. However, a man returning home late at night heard the sound of people approaching from the sea, and quickly hid himself in a bush at the side of the boreen. It was a moonlit night, and watching from his hiding place he saw a long line of African bearers carrying bundles of contraband passing by. He assumed because they wore native dress they were women, and in the light of the moon they looked dark blue, so the boreen became known as The Little Road of the Blue Women, later shortened to The Little Blue Road, or Botharin Gorm.

Whether or not the story is true, this coast is no stranger to that particular trade. The proximity of this corner of Ireland to the

Continent, and the large profits available, led many shipowners into the smuggling business over the centuries. The names of the smugglers were often commonly known, but they could not be arrested unless caught red-handed.

At the end of the boreen I came to a gate giving onto the public road, bearing the signs 'Beware of the Bull' and 'Keep Out'. I made my way down towards the beach, but almost immediately was set upon by a pack of dogs that issued from the farmyard beside the road. There were thirteen of them, mostly hungry-looking greyhounds, and all I could do was stand there calmly, not letting on I was terrified, while they ran circles around me, howling and barking fiercely. I had visions of one of them darting in to bite, followed by the whole pack descending on me in a bloody frenzy. Eventually, however, they began to lose interest, at least long enough for me to begin edging slowly down towards the beach, and escape. It was an uncomfortable experience, even surpassing my argument with the St. Bernard near Tramore!

Fornaght Strand is one of the last unspoiled beaches on the Waterford coast; in fact it is a great temptation to pass over it with little comment, to ensure it stays that way. Its saving grace, I suppose, is the fact that when the tide goes out, it is nothing but a strip of sand, because the dropping water exposes a wide expanse of stones, green seaweed and mud. But at full tide, in the morning when the sun gives the beach its full attention, the shelter, the calmness of the water, and the lush green surroundings make it a place apart.

As I crossed the little stream that drains the bramble-clad valley behind the beach, two vast Friesian cows were grazing beside the water. The water's edge was fringed with chequerboard flocks of oystercatchers waiting for the tide to drop and expose the mud banks; they took off as one, an explosion of black and white, sweeping away so close to the water's surface they might have been skating on it. They looped outwards and returned to the beach behind me, settling in unison again. A raven flew along the high tide line, searching out edible flotsam; alighting on the boulder-cliff at the far end of the beach it disturbed a heron who reluctantly flapped slowly to another strand.

Two fingers on high ground mirroring Credan Head extend

eastwards from the hinterland towards Waterford Harbour, one terminating three hundred yards short of the beach and the other, called Knockaveelish Head or Short Head, extending into the tide and forming the northern 'bookend' to Fornaght. With Credan, these 200-foot hills shelter the bay from southerly, northerly and westerly winds; only a hard easterly can cause discomfort on this beach.

I crossed the sand bank at the back of the beach to walk along the side of the marsh that stretches inland. Not far away a group of people were gathered, looking into a hole in the boggy ground. I stopped and leaned on my stick to watch what was going on. One of the hole gazers, seeing me arrive on the scene, came over.

'Hello', he said smiling, 'do you own the land around here?' He spoke with an English accent.

'Not at all', I replied. 'I'm just passing through.'

'I thought you were maybe one of the locals, and thought I should explain what we are at', he said, relaxing.

'Well I don't qualify, but I'm intrigued to know what you are up to!' I said.

The Englishman introduced himself as Tim Heap, from the University of Newcastle, and he had come to County Waterford with a group of students and staff to do some fieldwork on soils.

'We're glaciologists, and our particular expertise is in developing a picture of how our landscapes looked at various stages during the last ten thousand years since the Ice Age. By taking soil cores, we can retrieve and date remains of vegetable matter, seeds and pollen, which tell us what kinds of trees and plants thrived at different periods, and what kind of climatic conditions existed at the time.'

Tim and his companions were following up on an archaeological survey that had been carried out by his university and an American group the previous year, the key part of which involved walking the spring fields searching for flints or pottery shards or any other evidence of human occupation. After plotting the incidence of finds, certain locations looked like potential dig sites, and one of those was the land behind the beach at Fornaght.

An archaeological dig had taken place in the field at the back of the beach the previous year, during which the archaeologists were greatly excited by what they had unearthed. They were convinced that a stone platform-like formation was an early Stone Age settlement, which would have been the first to be found in this area. Every fragment that came out of the excavation became an obscure artefact, and they were looking forward to a winter writing up this dramatic discovery when one of Tim's glaciologists appeared on the dig. He identified the 'platform' as an interesting but common and natural glacial phenomenon!

We walked over to where three young men and two young women were gathered around a square trench in the bog behind the beach, assembling a set of aluminium tubes. The implement was stuck into the soil, and with extension pieces and a lot of elbow grease it was pushed down to a depth of about three metres. The tube was then withdrawn with a sucking noise, and opened up to expose a long dark cylinder of peat, which was divided into sections, bagged and documented.

'You can see some timber there', Tim said, pointing to dark streaks in the core. 'We'll be able to identify what species it was, and from the depth tell approximately when it grew here. Three metres down was probably the surface here six thousand years ago.'

I watched for a while longer while they worked on, taking cores from deeper and deeper in the bog, and then, thanking them for their explanations, I wished them an enjoyable stay in Ireland, and continued on my way.

There was no direct way from the beach up onto Knockaveelish Head, so I crossed a field to a boreen that meandered over the headland to Woodstown. It was overhung with dark purple buddleias and hollyhocks, around which played a cloud of red admirals, and was just wide enough for a car, leaving a linear lawn of green grass untouched along its centre. Along the right-hand side were located a few well-kept cottages, whose occupants had brought eucalyptus and palm trees to complement the native species; the hill at their back protected them from the north wind, and their south sides were open to the sun and the glorious view.

At the top of the hill, 200 feet above sea level, I left the boreen and crossed through a broad field along the crown of

Knockaveelish. Once again a panoramic view stopped me in my tracks, this time from the point of Hook to the south, to Mount Leinster, thirty-five miles inland to the north. Four thoroughbred mares that looked like racehorses were the only occupants of the field, and they stopped their grazing to watch me passing by. I thought to myself that a field such as this, on the top of the world (hereabouts anyway) was a fitting home for champions!

In a short time I reached a gorse and hawthorn-covered stone wall bisecting the headland, and climbing it, dropped down into a thick fox covert. Barely discernible paths, wending their way between bushes of broom tangled with wild roses, joined a series of small clearings. I followed one in the general direction of the point, and found it eventually disappeared into a twelve-inch diameter tunnel in thick gorse, to follow which I would have needed Alice's elixir! The paths obviously belonged to animals a lot smaller than me, probably badgers or rabbits, whose dried droppings could be seen scattered around each clearing. I had to fight my way through the prickly gorse, until I broke into more gentle bracken.

At last, the Scots pines that mark the point of Knockaveelish came into view against the deep blue sea. Hounded by a swarm of flies, and wielding my walking stick like a machete, I beat my way through the last brambles into the darkness and coolness of the wood that covers the northern slopes of the headland.

The wood was a dark green world, roofed in by thick canopies of beech and sycamore, supported by tall straight columns of tree trunks, the lower branches festooned with wreaths of ivy and woodbine. The floor of the wood was covered with a thick layer of crispy golden leaves from previous autumns, through which clumps of lush ferns rose. The pathway dropped steeply down under bridges formed by trees which had partially fallen, but remained propped by their neighbours, their death disguised by garlands of woodbine. Ferns and exposed roots provided handholds as I made my way downhill, cascading dust and leaves before me until I reached a moss-covered pathway running parallel with the promontory towards the mainland.

Once this was a good generous woodland path, but collapsing trees and a reduction in interest in keeping paths clear has led to it becoming an assault course, and every minute or so I had to climb over a fungi covered trunk or slip under one on my hands and knees. Great sprays of forest ferns clad the slopes above me, replacing the bluebells that clothe the place in early summer. As children, we knew this headland as Bluebell Valley, (although valley it certainly is not), and would come here to pick flowers and to play Cowboys and Indians. As I walked, I could just see the water below on the shore shining through the trees, and hear the splash and slosh of mullet playing the waters of the receding tide.

A deep shute or slide ran from the path almost vertically down to a rock outcrop at sea level that is, or used to be, a favourite fishing place; it was here, with help and a borrowed rod, I caught my first fish when I was ten, a five pound salmon bass. The thrill of it, the bursting pride I felt, I can remember to this day.

The path improved as I moved inland and the trees cleared to my right, with one great oak tree framing a glimpse of the glorious white beach of Woodstown to the north. The reduction in density of trees gave the sun a chance to break through, dappling the ground and sparkling off the shiny holly leaves and ivy. From the edge of the wood, I could see in the water thirty feet below the mullet I had heard splashing earlier. They were large grey-blue fish with silver sides and bellies, clearly visible as they circled and chased each other. The shallows were full of the fish, rooting in the muddy bottom like pigs, and creating substantial bow waves as they moved. Shoals like this have always run into Woodstown with the tide in hot weather and often I swam right up to individual fish, as they hung at the surface, their dorsal fins disguised in a clump of floating seaweed. Not highly regarded today for eating, they were once popular when taken fresh, as this excerpt from *The Field Book* of 1833 suggests:

> When used immediately after being taken, the fish is excellent; carriage even for a short distance, injures it. Dr. Blotch recommends oil and lemon juice to be used with it at table. Vinegar, with parsley and melted butter, is better — 'probatum est' . . . from its spawn an inferior kind of caviar, called 'botargo' is prepared.

Seaweed-covered rocks, exposed by the falling tide, were immediately occupied by flocks of oystercatchers and long-legged waders, looking like a Tunnicliffe painting, awaiting their evening meal.

The track I was following soon reached the public road, and I turned down for Woodstown strand through a tunnel of tall, old, majestic beeches. In places the narrow road is cut from the bedrock, whose smooth sides rise ten feet, before it comes out into the light again at the southern end of the strand.

Woodstown is at its best on sunny weekday mornings, when it is often deserted, and the early sun is poised over the Wexford coast on the far side of the harbour; or on summer evenings when there is a very high tide, and the mullet, lulled by the heat, are hanging listlessly under the doubtful cover of a piece of seaweed on the calm sea surface.

Even in the height of winter, Woodstown is difficult to beat, when you can crunch your way for a bracing two-mile walk over the bleached white cockleshells with only a stooping heron and a half-dozen oystercatchers for company. A few lucky people have houses on the beach; some have been there since the last century, and others look as if they have grown gradually and unobtrusively from tiny wooden holiday huts.

On a wooded prominence at the southern end of the beach stands Ballyglan House, built by one of the Carew family towards the end of the eighteenth century, its siting as carefully considered as the proportions of its facade. Admiring a bay mare that grazed in the pasture below the house, I crossed a stream which tumbled onto the beach from a tunnel under the road.

Near the high tide mark, I came across the corpse of a huge jellyfish, stranded as the tide swiftly withdrew. The translucent body of the monster measured fully one foot six inches across, and when I turned him over with my foot, a cluster of pearl-coloured tentacles were revealed that must have hung down almost three feet below the water's surface. Farther on down the beach, I saw another and another, and stretching off into the distance many more, lining the high water mark. Coming towards me along the beach was Paul Tritscheler, an old family friend. Paul has been walking this coast for fifty years, and there is little he misses, so I asked him had he seen this jellyfish phenomenon before.

'When I came here in the twenties as a boy I remember the beach being covered with jellyfish,' he said slowly as he thought about it. 'There would be so many, the beach would stink for weeks. There were also at other times of the year shoals of fish stranded regularly when the tide went out. They were called goat mackerel, just like the mackerel you'd see today, except for great spines down his back.'

He told me of his holidays in those days, spent in a nearby house overlooking the beach, and how the great weir, some of whose poles still stretch out from the beach towards the Wexford coast, was operated. He remembered baskets full of fish of all kinds being taken from the nets after every tide.

'I better be moving along', he said; 'see you again,' and he strode off down the strand at a steady pace, leaving me with a very graphic picture of Woodstown in another time.

Halfway down the beach, summery in its Bermudan pink, is Weir House, a rambling informal building with an uninterrupted view across to Wexford. Nearby, the five-foot cauldron that was used to boil the pitch to coat the nets for the great weir can still be seen.

Farther along the beach stands the Saratoga Bar, a pleasant and friendly watering place. Saratoga is not what could be called a local place-name, and is said to have been suggested to the original owner by a returned emigrant from the United States, who thought the place had a remarkable resemblance to Saratoga Springs, a spa in the State of New York.

Inland, a few hundred yards from the beach stands Woodstown House, originally the seat of the Carew family, who owned much of the land and built almost all the houses in the area. One Lady Carew, who was born in 1799, attended the ball given in Brussels on the night before the Battle of Waterloo, and was still recounting the story up to her death in 1902, having lived through the entire eighteenth century!

Beyond the Saratoga Bar I took to the road as it turned inland and mounted Giant's Hill, where, according to the Ordnance Map, there should be an old rath or tumulus. I found no trace of it, only fields strewn with black plastic-sheeted silage mounds, speckled with blue and white fertiliser bags filled with sand to weigh them down.

At the top of the hill the high stone walls and star-fort corners of what remains of the notorious Geneva Barracks rise incongruously from the fields. The barracks fell into disuse and most of the buildings were demolished in the 1820s. The history of the place before it became a barracks is fascinating.

In 1781 an insurrection occurred in the city-state of Geneva which was ruled by an alliance that included France and the states of Zurich and Berne. The majority of its population of 24,000 wanted their independence. The French and Swiss armies quickly surrounded the city and laid siege to it, joined later by the forces of the King of Sardinia, who also had an interest in the affair. After prolonged negotiations, the rebellious citizens were allowed to leave with all their belongings. Some settled in Brussels and others near Lake Constance, but the rest scattered throughout Europe, seeking sanctuary.

In Ireland, restrictions on foreign trade were removed in 1780, and legislative independence from England was granted in 1782. The climate was right for economic advancement, and the country had developed a reputation as a sympathetic haven for refugees, particularly if they were of the Protestant persuasion. A group of wealthy, skilled and homeless Genevan artisans applied for asylum in Ireland. The advantages of a community of enlightened Protestants importing their industrial skills and money (many of the Genevans had considerable investments) into Ireland were at once seen, and the assent of George III was sought and received. After considerable discussions and political lobbying, a decision was made to settle the Genevans in a newly built town on the southern side of Waterford Harbour, and the Irish Parliament voted a grant of £50,000 towards the project.

The site selected for the new town was a substantial tract of

140

land with access to shipping at Passage East, about a mile distant. In July 1783 a deputation of Genevans arrived in Waterford to assist in planning the new town. They were people of exceptional ability and accomplishments. Amongst them was a M. Clavière, a talented entrepreneur and businessman who later became the French Minister of Finance, and a master watchmaker by the name of M. Chalons, who like Peter the Great had walked and worked his way around Europe for years, extending his knowledge and skills; he spoke most languages, including English, with no detectable accent.

James Gandon, architect of Dublin's Custom House, was commissioned to plan New Geneva, as it was to be called, and he laid out the new town on a gridiron plan with a subtly curved Bath-like terrace terminating in churches. An academy or university was also included in the plans; it was to have 44 professors and masters to lecture on arts and sciences and an extensive library.

Building work began late in 1783 on the houses and workshops, and the Gold Standard, which had stood since 1729, was altered to suit the Genevan goldsmiths. There was to be an assay office at New Geneva, and three new marks were devised: a harp with bar, a plume of two feathers and a unicorn's head. For the first time in Ireland punches on the Genevan style were to be used, which had an indented impression rather than a relief one to prevent alterations being made.

Last-minute problems arose about the details of the charter to be granted to the new town, and suddenly the whole scheme, even at this advanced stage, fell through. The reasons were never fully explained. It is thought that the Genevans had become unreasonable in their demands, looking for privileges and freedoms that were impossible for the authorities to grant. Another theory is that the Corporation of Waterford became jealous, and insisted that New Geneva should be under its jurisdiction. The Lord Lieutenant, who had championed the Genevans' cause, had been recalled a short time before, and his successor, the Duke of Rutland, had little interest in the scheme.

It is difficult to imagine what the results would have been if history had taken a different course and a strong community of wealthy and liberal Genevans had established themselves here.

Apart from the political consequences, the subsequent effect on the economy of the district, combined with the success of the crystal glass industry founded in 1786, would have been considerable.

A total of £30,000 had been spent on dwellings and other buildings for the new town at the time of the collapse of the scheme, and they became the headquarters of the Waterford militia when it was formed in 1793. Later, the massive defensive wall encompassing the whole place was built. The influx of a large population of rough conscripts into this quiet coastal area had a detrimental effect on the locality, which, had the Genevans stayed, might have been enjoying considerable prosperity.

The older houses on the road between Geneva and Passage have no windows facing onto the road, an architectural feature said to have developed due to fear of drunken yeomanry returning to the barracks after an evening in the night spots of Passage!

After the 1798 Rebellion, Geneva became a prison to contain some of the huge number of rebels who had been rounded up; within fifteen years a place that had been set aside as a sanctuary for foreign revolutionaries had become a notorious jail for the native variety. At one stage there were 1,200 prisoners within the walls of Geneva, and overcrowding led to 'violent fevers and infectious disorders'. The local Protestant vicar, Rev. M. Roberts (son of John Roberts, architect of many of the finer buildings of the period in Waterford), reported to his sorrow that some of those imprisoned were Protestants, and he visited them regularly, 'cheerfully . . .at the hazard of my life on which a wife and nine children' depended for support! The hazard to his life may have been as much due to the militia as the prisoners; one report tells of a woman visitor being stripped by them and tossed high into the air again and again in a blanket. The terrified and screaming woman could be seen by those outside the walls as she reached the high point of her flight.

There were many dramatic attempts to escape from the barracks, including the construction of a tunnel under the walls which failed at the last minute. The clay from the tunnel was taken 'off the premises' in true Colditz style under the dresses of the prisoners' wives. One prisoner made a successful escape, concealed under a heap of horse manure being taken out of the barracks by cart.

Stories and songs referring to the legendary Croppy Boy mention Geneva Barracks, and indeed many 'Croppies', so-called because of their short hairstyle, were executed there after 1798. A number of graves in the area purport to be that of the Croppy Boy of the song; two of them were extant in the ruins of Crook Church, one used to be pointed out in the shadow of the barracks wall, and a sign on the gable of a house in Passage indicated that he was laid to rest there.

Geneva Barracks was abandoned by the military in the early 1830s and changed hands a number of times before being sold to a Mr Galway for a nominal sum. He had most of the houses demolished and the material shipped by sea to Dungarvan to erect 'cabins for his tenantry'.

One of the few that appeared to benefit from the 'New Geneva' episode was the local Catholic priest, Father Hearn. He lived at the time in a small house at Carey's Bridge, just beyond New Geneva. The new town was to be substantially greater in extent than the present barracks area of twelve acres, and Father Hearn did not relish being surrounded by Protestants, so he petitioned the government to exchange his house for land further at Knockparson. It is very possible that he also offered to keep the locals 'quiet' during the disruptions that were to come, because he ended up getting a full twenty acres from the government,(a strange thing during the Penal times), on which he built a substantial house — Crook Villa. During the most notorious period at Geneva Barracks in 1798, Father Hearn wrote that the officers in charge were remarkable 'for their attention to every principle of honour, justice and humanity'! In return for this praise, the militia officers presented him with a silver snuffbox.

The hamlet of Crook is today a gathering of modern bungalows dominated by a grey two-storey parochial house and a severe neo-gothic church. A little boy on a BMX confirmed for me that the overgrown track beside the church would take me down to the seashore again and I could walk to Passage that way, but because he thought it was possible I would drown in the incoming tide, he suggested I continue by the road! He also recommended that I should view the inside of the church, which he said

had been 'done up'. In order not to disappoint this budding Bord
Failte director, I walked down the gravel path to the entrance
porch. He watched me carefully from the saddle of his BMX until
I did so.

The porch must have been built in a hurry some years ago
when the draught from a cold west wind gave the parish priest a
chill. The stone commemoration plaque on the gable has been
partly obliterated by the porch being plonked regardless against
the gable. With this evidence of philistinism, I was not expecting
much of the interior, and was pleasantly surprised. The fine, flat
nineteenth-century ceiling in square panels had been carefully
repainted in a floral Iesus Hominum Salvator design, and the
walls were sensitively toned to give the place a peaceful ambience.

When I left the church I met a gang of young children in a

state of high excitement. One of them was carrying a recently deceased wagtail.

'Look what we found, Mister' they chorused.

'Will it poison me, Mister?' the lad carrying the bird wanted to know.

I assured him it would not, but it might be a good idea to give the willy wagtail a decent funeral without delay.

'That's what we're doing,' the mourners exclaimed with relish.

'In my back,' the undertaker proudly added.

As I went on my way along the road towards Passage, the cortege was stopped by an older girl, who squeaked in horror at the sight of the corpse. Before turning the corner out of earshot, I heard the indignant retort: 'The man said it's not poisonous!'

Reaching the brow of a hill a few minutes later, the hamlet of Ballyhack, with its tall Templar castle, came into view on the far side of the river, and the road began to descend towards the grey slated roofs of Passage East. In the broad expanse of river between these two places, convoys of many tall-masted merchant ships would gather during the 1790s, before sailing out of the safety of the harbour under the protection of the Royal Navy. During that decade and into the nineteenth century, French privateers prowled the high seas waiting to pounce on and capture unarmed merchant ships.

As I descended into Passage I could see a herd of shaggy feral goats moving about on the cliffs that rise sharply from the back of the village. It is surprising to see the animals coexisting so closely with humans.

Passage East has undergone a transformation since the car-ferry service connecting east Waterford with Wexford was inaugurated in the early 1980s. Before then it was a sleepy and decaying little village, its former importance as an embarkation port for travellers sailing east and as a packet station, a thing of the past. Now it is a vibrant, colourful village, its fine old houses refurbished and smartly painted. Many who arrive here in summertime are visitors from the Continent or Britain, off the ferries at Rosslare, and Passage gives them an introduction to the county that Waterford people can be proud of.

Passage has always been a place of arrivals and departures:

many of the figures who decided the course of Irish history came to Ireland or left via Passage. It was near here in 1171 that Henry II landed with 500 knights and 400 men-at-arms, to ensure his interests were looked after by Richard de Clare, also known as Strongbow, who had masterminded the first Norman landing in Ireland two years before.

Henry's son, John, arrived some years later, accompanied by a large retinue which included the historian Giraldus Cambrensis, to 'sow his wild oats' in Ireland. It is said that he feasted so well on Passage salmon that he almost died! He returned again as King John in 1210 and stayed for some months in Waterford.

Nearly two hundred years later Richard II sailed up Waterford harbour with a force the size of which had never before or probably since been seen in the area. Son of the the Black Prince, Richard was in line for the coveted title 'King of the Holy Roman Empire', but the Irish chiefs' disregard of English laws and rule was known all over Europe and was an embarrassment to him. Partly to regain his stature in the eyes of the European princes, Richard landed near Passage in October 1394 with a huge and colourful army of 34,000 men to seek or force the allegiance of his Irish subjects.

As this military extravaganza moved northwards, it was constantly and painfully harassed by the forces of Art MacMurrough Kavanagh, King of Leinster, whose guerrilla tactics soon had Richard's army looking less colourful. Eventually the Irish decided that it would be politic to offer allegiance to the English king, and MacMurrough was knighted by Richard!

Richard II again sailed up Waterford Harbour in 1399, to attempt to subjugate the Irish chiefs, particularly MacMurrough. This time he employed a scorched earth policy and press-ganged the Irish peasantry into cutting a way for his set-piece army through the deep woodlands in pursuit of the Irish. MacMurrough's men again wore down the English with lightning attacks, and cut off their supply line. Eventually the beleaguered army fought its way, starving and exhausted, to the Wicklow coast, where they were provisioned by sea. From there they struggled on to Dublin, where Richard received word that his kingdom was under threat at home from his cousin Henry. He sailed with what was left of his army for Wales, but he was too late. Deposed by Henry, he spent his last days a prisoner in Pontefract Castle.

Another English king to pass through Passage was the exhausted and defeated James II, who is said to have arrived here a few days after the battle of the Boyne to embark for France. The story is told that as he stood awaiting a punt to take him out to his shop at anchor in midstream, his broad-brimmed plumed hat blew off into the river. A young aide immediately came to his side and presented him with his own hat.

'Come,' the defeated king said, half-bitterly, half-ironically, 'I have lost a kingdom in Ireland, but I have gained a hat!'

A hundred and fifty years later, Queen Victoria, on a tour of the British Isles in the royal yacht, spent the night at anchor off Passage. She noted in her diary the picturesque surroundings, and the fact that they had eaten 'excellent' salmon, for which Passage East was famous.

I walked out of the sunshine, into the comfortable gloom of the Farleigh Bar, for a glass of stout.

There were a surprising number of mid-afternoon customers at the long bar, and a spirited game of darts was in progress. Although there were three or four distinct groups of drinkers gathered at the counter, at times the conversation became general, with anyone and everyone throwing in their comments.

With the All Ireland Final imminent, there was knowledgeable discussion about the relative merits of the teams, and about Gaelic games in general.

'Cork and Kilkenny are by far the two best counties in Ireland for Gaelic, and d'ye know why!' one of the debaters demanded of the customers at large.

'They're the only parts of the country where you never see kids without a hurley in their hands, that's why.'

'That's only at Irish games,' retorted an older man at the darkest end of the bar. What about soccer and so on?'

'Hurling and Gaelic football aren't Irish games,' a third man interjected from the corner of the room.

The whole assembly turned and regarded him with derision.

He slowly drank from his pint, waiting masterfully for the bait to be taken.

A ruddy-faced youth rose like an unsuspecting trout. 'Whadaya mean, hurling and Gaelic are not Irish? Of course they're Irish,' he piped.

'Hurling was invented in China over two thousand years ago', the scholar condescendingly explained, gesturing to the landlord for another pint. 'They used to play however,' he continued slowly, 'not with a leather ball, but with the heads of their enemies.' This brought roars of derisive disbelief and disagreement from all sides. 'And what about Gaelic football?' someone shouted.

'Sure it's well known,' the sage teased, 'football was being played in Egypt three thousand years before Ireland existed!'

I left under the confusion that reigned after this announcement, leaving behind the atmosphere of smoke and laughter, and made my way down to the Ferry slipway.

The figure of a man dressed completely in yellow oilskin material, his face covered by a mask, was hovering about the jetty, wielding a sort of ray gun device. He looked incongruous on such a hot day in a peaceful Irish village. It seemed that he was just keeping the slipway clear of seaweed to prevent cars coming off the ferry from skidding. I wondered what else was being affected in the river by his spray gun.

Gently dominating the village of Passage from the impressive crag that rises almost vertically above the furthest row of houses from the river are the remains of St Anne's Church. Built in 1746 on the site of a more ancient church, St. Anne's was up to a few years ago a fine example of rural Georgian architecture, listed in the 1970s by An Foras Forbartha as worthy of preservation. It was sold by the Church of Ireland in 1978, and has now been converted into a dwelling house.

As I left Passage, climbing up the long hill on a road carved out of the cliffside, the breadth of the Three Sisters, the combined Barrow, Nore and Suir, became clearer, for between here and the next village on the river bank the watercourse must be over a mile wide in places.

A little more than a mile-and-a-half outside Passage on the Waterford road, a sign indicating a Picnic Area leads to one of the finest footpaths I have walked along this coast. It is an old 'green road', which existed long before the present main road was even thought of, the direct route to Cheekpoint from Passage until such a direct route became unnecessary. It was good to be off the tarmac again and on soft green grass. The boreen became narrower and narrower, greener and greener, and more perfumed as it ascended to a high point over 300 feet above the surface of the river below.

I sat on a narrow slab of old red sandstone that projected out almost over the water, providing a most spectacular natural viewing station. Brandon Hill and the Blackstairs to the north acted as a book-end to the rolling Wexford landscape that terminated in the sliver of the Hook Peninsula. In the near distance, the river swept broadly upstream from Passage to narrow as it rounded the bend at Cheekpoint. Martins zoomed over my hand with inches to spare as I sat there, heady with the perfume of bracken and heather. A long way below me two fishermen in a punt were wrestling with a long salmon net, strung out on a necklace of floats across the river.

Reluctantly leaving this most enjoyable of viewing points, I followed the boreen downhill, rejoining the public road briefly, but left it again as soon as possible, and dropped down through thick mature woodland to the river bank, near the remains of an ancient pier of massive stones.

The chimneys of the ghastly oil-fired power station that violates the river bank opposite Cheekpoint soon came into view as I walked northwards along the shore, but the rising tide forced me to retreat inland before I had travelled far. Passing a strange little conical-roofed round tower with gothic windows, I reached the main road into Cheekpoint village. I asked a man sitting on a wall if the little tower was very old, and was told that it had been built in the last century as a folly by a doting father for his spoiled daughter. This sounded most intriguing, but my informant unfortunately knew no more of the story.

If one can ignore the monstrosity across the river, something which is very difficult to do, Cheekpoint is a picturesque place, located at the meeting of the Suir, approaching from the west, and the combined Barrow and Nore, coming from the north under the railway viaduct. It is a good place to be on a fine summer's evening, when the river waters double the beauty of sunset. The

Barrow comes all the way from the Slieve Bloom Mountains, 'the middle of Ireland', by way of Portarlington, Kildare, Athy and Carlow; while the Nore, rising near the Devil's Bit, graces Kilkenny and Thomastown on its way to meet the Barrow above New Ross. Here at Cheekpoint they join the Suir, to form the broad and deep Waterford Harbour.

The name Cheekpoint apparently comes from the Gaelic Poinnte na Sige, meaning the Point of the Streak, referring, it is said, to a long trail or streak in the flowing river caused by a rock or other obstruction. I prefer to think that Sige derived from the Gaelic word for fairies; the Point of the Fairies has a far more romantic ring! For nearly thirty years, spanning the end of the eighteenth and the beginning of the nineteenth centuries, the name of the village was changed to Bolton, after Cornelius Bolton, a local landowner. In two places along the road to Waterford, before the Brass Cock and near Passage Road in Newtown, finely carved milestones dating from the period can still be found, referring to 'Bolton or Cheekpoint'.

As part of his effort to bring the Industrial Revolution to this part of the world, Bolton used his considerable political influence to have the main Milford-Waterford Packet Station located at the village. It was thought it would be quicker to get the mail to Waterford on horseback than have the mail boat continue up the Suir to the city, especially when the tides and winds were not favourable. For five years following 1787, this system was followed, until it was decided that Passage would be an even better location, and the Station was moved there in 1792.

Passing McAlpine's Bar and Restaurant, where having to perch on stools and eat off small bar tables had never kept customers from queuing to partake of the exceptionally good seafood, I walked across the road to finish the day's walk at Cheekpoint's little pier.

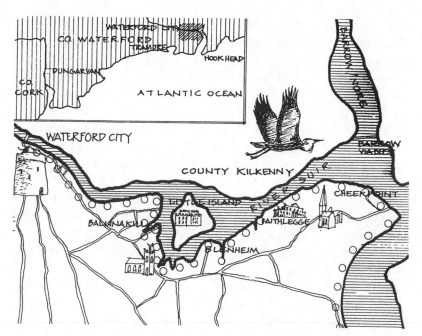

CHEEKPOINT TO WATERFORD BRIDGE

Although Waterford was only ten miles away now, I was unaware that circumstances would dictate that the time it would take me to get there would be measured in weeks rather than hours. I walked out of Cheekpoint on a glorious summer's morning, joined for this stretch by my brother Tom with his dog Prince, and an old friend from Clare, Dick Cronin. The Barrow Viaduct gleamed silver across the water, connecting County Kilkenny with County Wexford. For a short while after it was built in the early twentieth century, this was the longest viaduct in the British Isles. The tide was just out far enough to expose the seaweed-shrouded stumps of old weir posts, each providing a perch for a seagull, patiently awaiting the emergence of the mud-banks that deliver to them each day a fresh meal.

Beside a road that headed steeply uphill and inland stood a tall, five-bayed, three-storey Georgian house in red brick. Still partially roofed and in reasonable repair, this pile, quite out of scale with everything else in Cheekpoint, is what remains of Cornelius Bolton's Packet Station Inn. In its short career in the tourist business it failed to gain a high reputation; one visitor from England wrote in 1800, 'Cheekpoint, a very dirty, dear, bad Inn, only staid there to breakfast, or more properly speaking to dine on bad bread and tea'.

Passing a little terrace of houses beyond what might have been the quay built for the packet, we made our way uphill through a dew wet meadow roughly following a right-of-way marked on my 6-inch map. Near the 200-foot contour we passed a small whitewashed cottage in a most secluded location, and climbed through another meadow, whose heavy herbal scent was almost intoxicating. Soon there was no trace of a right-of-way or track, so we kept on hacking towards the woods that clothe the steep riverside for a mile upstream, and through which I knew a good path ran. Tom had predicted a hot day ahead and was wearing shorts. As we came to the sixth patch of nettles, he asked if we could follow each field of nettles with a field of dockleaves! Clouds of meadow browns and tortoiseshells patrolled the meadow around us and the views to the north and west across the river were exceptional, with the Blackstairs and Comeragh mountains forming the backdrops.

Glazing Wood, which follows the river here for about a mile, consists mainly of recent trees and rhododendrons, because the old deciduous wood that originally covered the hill was cut down during the last war to provide fuel for Faithlegge House, then a De La Salle seminary. The pathway, which runs through the woods at a height of 300 feet above the river, is a pleasure to follow at any time of the year. As we entered the gloom of the wood, purple blooms of the rhododendrons were pinpointed dramatically in places by shafts of sunlight, and the river could be seen sparkling through a lace of foliage down to our right. The pine needle pathway led us past frequent openings in the trees, giving us extensive vistas of the river and its banks, stitched by the remains of numerous fish weirs.

Fish weirs were introduced into Ireland by the Norman Cistercian and Benedictine monks, and the rights to some of the weirs remaining in the rivers are very ancient. Some of those seaweed-covered poles that can be seen protruding in lines from the river Suir are probably a couple of hundred years old, and the ownership rights go back to Norman times, when they were often in the gift of the king. The weirs we were looking at would have taken a wide variety of fish, including codling, ling, plaice, cod, megs, dabs and lemon sole, salmon, trout and bass.

Halfway through Glazing Wood a vaulted structure led off the path and out ten or fifteen feet onto a railed platform jutting from the cliff, with a spectacular 180 degree view up and down the river. We discussed what the purpose of this construction could have been, and Dick came up with what appeared to be the best suggestion: that it was probably a toll belfry, where ships proceeding up river were noted as they passed, and a toll bell, which would originally have been mounted on the arch, would be rung.

As the western end of the wood we came out to a fragrant meadow. Prince went bounding ahead, glad to be in the open again. As we walked, we picked up the sickly sweet smell of something dead, and before long we came across the week-old corpse of a badger. From the teeth in his skull he must have been in his prime when he died. Tom said it was unusual to see a dead badger that had not been killed on the road. I would have liked to have had his fine skull for my mantelpiece, but even if I had been prepared to detach it, and put up with the smell, I would have been on my own for the rest of the day!

Crossing a road, we made our way across a field to the riverside and carried on by its edge. The pasture and woodland of the 300 acre Little Island came into sight before us, dividing the Suir into two channels, and beyond it we could see the construction cranes on the Ardkeen hospital. Ardkeen is only a couple of miles from the centre of Waterford, so this was a momentous sighting; my coastal walk was nearing its end.

County Kilkenny was only a quarter-of-a-mile away now, and

substantial houses could be seen surrounded by sheltering trees; straight across from us was an extensive Georgian farmhouse with the unusual name of 'Glasshouse'.

After crossing a couple of fields and turning inland to avoid mudbanks, we entered another wood called Willow Wood, where foxgloves grew to amazing heights seeking the sun. We turned south-east and followed a neck of woods towards Faithlegge House, and suddenly there it was, rising out of terraced gardens of overgrown powder blue hydrangeas — a great grey pedimented pile that had more bulk than elegance.

The house and demesne were unoccupied at the time we passed by, and I was later told that they had been 'seized' by the banks after a major scheme for the development of the place as a leisure centre had foundered almost before it started. The plan was for the place to be turned into a luxury hotel, complete with a first-rate golf course that was said to have been designed by Jack Nicklaus. The bulldozers had begun to tear up the grounds and uproot the fine old trees for the roads and carparks when, for some reason, the project fell through, leaving a forest of burnt fingers. Where there had been extensive parklands with fine stands of beech, oak, lime and chestnut, we found a place that looked like a battlefield, with great holes in the earth and heaps of twisted roots and branches. The house was still intact, but the gravel driveway and forecourt were being overcome by a sea of green clover. The trees immediately around the house, great limes and maples that must have been planted by Cornelius Bolton about 1783, also still survived.

Faithlegge was then a lot smaller than it is today, consisting of the seven-bay central block without wings, and was most probably a far more elegant building of Georgian simplicity.

The Faithlegge area is first mentioned in written annals when the Aylward family, Bristol merchants and ship owners, were granted lands in the area by Henry II, probably in payment for providing the king and his army with ships for his Irish excursion in 1171.

The advance guard of the Aylwards, as was the Norman fashion of the time, probably built the motte and bailey, the remains of which can still be seen at Moat Farmhouse, about half a mile to

the east of Faithlegge. When they became accepted or tolerated by the local Irish, and persuaded themselves that a living could be made here, they built a castle near the motte, and settled into the area. For almost five hundred years the family prospered, keeping in touch with their business interests in England, and maintaining their Catholic faith through the Reformation. The John Aylward of Cromwell's time is said not only to have known the Protector personally, but to have loaned him money at some stage. Cromwell must have held Aylward in high regard, because before he sailed for Ireland with 20,000 men to reduce the Irish to submission, he sent a message to him offering to bypass Faithlegge if he would cease to practice his religion publicly. Aylward, having a fair idea of what was in store, was tempted by this offer, but apparently his wife read him the riot act and he refused it. After Waterford surrendered to Ireton's forces in 1649, a detachment under a Captain Bolton was sent to storm Aylward's castle, and after a brief siege, during which cannon were used, the Aylwards surrendered. Within days the family had been sent westward with their goods and livestock, to make a new life west of the Shannon.

A few years later, it was decreed that Captain Bolton and his men were to be 'satisfied' (for arrears of pay) with lands in Tipperary and Waterford. Bolton got Faithlegge and had an additional 2,834 acres confirmed to him by Charles II, and built a house at nearby Ballycanvan. He was reputed to have preached from the pulpit in Waterford Cathedral in jackboots, and during a stormy political career, was twice mayor of the city.

By the time of Arthur Young's visit to Ballycanvan House in 1776, the incumbent Bolton was a liberal, reforming landlord who drained the land, built roads and encouraged 'his poor cottier tenantry . . . this is the way to give the Catholics right ideas'. The grander Faithlegge House was built by his son, Cornelius, who was a more ambitious man. He managed to arrange for the Waterford to Milford package to use Cheekpoint as its station on the Irish side, and had visions of the place joining the Industrial Revolution, as the cottage-based industries he established there expanded. For five years the mail station brought a measure of prosperity to the village, but in 1792 the authorities decided that Passage was a better location and in that year it was transferred. Cornelius Bolton eventually got into financial difficulties, and by 1818, overextended on many fronts, he faced financial ruin. Faithlegge House and lands had to be sold, ending over 150 years of Bolton dominance in the area.

The next owners of Faithlegge were the Powers, a Catholic family who became known as the richest commoners in Ireland. Nicholas Mahon Power was a benefactor of Brother Ignatius Rice, who founded the Christian Brothers, helping to finance the first schools in Waterford, and strongly supported Daniel O'Connell, who called Power 'the right kind of agitator'! Within two years of his death his son Patrick completely renovated the house, having it refaced in the style of the time, and adding the wings and portico that can be seen today.

Patrick was renowned as a great huntsman, and was regarded as remarkable in that he never swore at his hounds or fellow huntsmen!

In 1936 the house was sold to the De La Salle Brothers, who set up a seminary, and they were the lords of Faithlegge for over forty years. The future of the place when I passed by seemed uncertain; it would be a shame to see the demesne and house fall into decay.

Leaving Faithlegge House, we followed the forest track back to the riverside through a more recent wood of well-spaced young conifers, where we found the stone-built quay and boathouse that used to serve the demesne. The quay at one time was a substantial structure made from great blocks of sandstone, but the river had undermined the part nearest the shore, and what remained was a grass and wildflower-covered island. The sad-looking boathouse was roofless, overgrown and in dangerous condition, but with a little imagination one could picture the scene here in bygone days. The Powers had relations who owned Bellevue, a great house on the opposite bank, and if a good hunt was under way, a signal to that effect would be sent by semaphore across the river. Patrick Power, never one to miss a good hunt, would don his distinctive green hunting jacket and take the pinnace to the Kilkenny bank to join in.

Further on through the wood, we passed what must have once been a gamekeeper's cottage, now invaded by the undergrowth, the cast iron range in the tiny kitchen and the bedstead the only recognisable artefacts to escape total decay.

We left the subdued light of the wood and, once more in the bright sunshine, walked along the narrow margin between the trees and the Suir, startling a flock of curlews. Extending out from the grassy mudflats was yet another fish weir, the pole tops occupied by a few common gulls who disdainfully ignored us and watched the curlews sweep out across the river. This section of riverside wood is called 'Oak Wood' on the ordnance maps, and although practically all the oaks were cut down during World War II for fuel, a number of small stunted examples remain scattered throughout the modern coniferous mix.

Oak Wood is interrupted by the broad estuary of the Woodland Pill, a stream draining the Faithlegge peninsula into the Suir. The estate road that ran through the woods, more or less parallel to the river, once crossed the Pill over a substantial stone bridge. Today the bridge, after years of neglect, has been reduced to a heap of stones gradually being scattered by the river and the Pill, but there was just enough of it left to form stepping stones, and we crossed easily. The Pill created a picturesque clearing in the woodland extending inland, and nearby some more of the Faithlegge estate buildings barely protruded from the undergrowth and dog roses that had enveloped them.

The track we had been following through the woods now became a 'green road' that ran through more mature trees parallel to and above the river. Framed in a stand of monkey puzzle trees here is Woodlands House, originally a dower house of Faithlegge, and beyond it we came to the stark and substantial ruins of Ballycanvan House, the original home of the Bolton family. In a very dilapidated condition and without its roof, the main section had two stories over a basement, with brick-lined windows; attached to this section was a three-storey simpler block with very thick walls.

We climbed into this older part of the house for a closer look, and Dick pointed out features such as wall thickness and wickerwork plaster reinforcement on the soffit of an arch, suggesting

158

that this part of Ballycanvan was built before the end of the seventeenth century as a fortified house. As we moved delicately around the fragile ruin, we came across some cut-stonework that seemed to bear this out.

The grandfather of Thomas Francis Meagher, Irish patriot, prisoner in Van Diemen's Land, leader of the Irish Brigade in the American Civil War, and governor of the State of Montana, lived in Ballycanvan House early in the nineteenth century.

Beyond Ballycanvan House, we followed the green road through a sea of tall ragweed until, clambering over a pair of ancient decaying gates, we found ourselves on the public road once again. After the coolness of the woods it was hot and airless in the open, and when we came to a picturesque pub called Meades, crouching under a viaduct-like bridge on the Waterford-Passage road, it was impossible to carry on without stopping for refreshment.

Meades is the last remaining building still doing business in what must have been a bustling crossroads village in the nineteenth century. On the maps the place is called Halfway House, presumably halfway from Waterford to the Packet Station at Passage. Across the road from the pub are the ruins of the local smithy, while nearby, almost taken over by undergrowth, are the remains of Brook Lodge Corn Mill, both of which were carrying on business within living memory. Behind Meades pub and across the Ballycanvan Pill is a double limekiln, a sign that although the Pill now has only a trickle of water, in the last century it was navigable by barges up to this point. I was puzzled however, by another ruined building near the limekiln, a circular structure that could have been a tower house, except it seemed to be constructed of more modern stonework.

The grassy terraced grounds around the pub are furnished with an informal scatter of rustic seats and tables, and it was at one of these, under the shade of an elder bush, that we washed down sandwiches with delicious glasses of chilled beer.

When we got up to move on, Tom noticed that Prince was limping, and when he knelt and lifted one of the dog's forepaws he found a deep slit across one of the pads, probably caused by broken glass. Tom decided he could go no further, but would have to arrange to be picked up and bring the dog to the vet. The lunchtime beer and the heat of the afternoon sun had in any case put us all in a very relaxed state of mind, and instead of carrying on, Dick and I were happy to curtail the walk, to be taken up again on a later date.

In spite of my being anxious to complete the last few miles, it was not until a few weeks later that I was able to take up where I had left off at Meades. At ten o'clock on a morning that promised a much different climate than when I had set out from Cheekpoint, I restarted at Meades with two friends I had managed to persuade to join me, Peter Carroll and Frank Clarke, both local men who knew the area well.

Peter started the day well by solving the mystery of the round tower just across the stream, telling me it was an ice house.

'It is built like a great circular cavity wall,' he explained.

'Two walls — you can see where the outer one is broken away there — with insulation between the two, and ice was collected during the winter, and packed with brine into the building with big hunks of meat; that's how they kept the meat and other perishables.'

Halfway House is almost a mile inland from the Suir, and we made our way towards the river along the west bank of the Pill, disturbing a large family of pheasants in the long grass. They scattered swiftly, the camouflaged plumage of the slender young birds rendering them instantly invisible in the undergrowth.

Before long, the going became very boggy along the stream side and we had to cut up into the fields just above the foreshore. Unlike the easily negotiable hedges of the coast, in this part of the country they are substantial; often as much as eight feet wide, and almost inpenetrable with bushes, trees and the ubiquitous bramble. Luckily, most of these hedges had a generous opening here or there leading into the next field. The ones that did not, Peter explained, were usually 'bound's ditches', forming the boundary to a farmer's land. Peter's experience as a pheasant shooter, and Frank's as a beagler, became very useful as we navigated our way across the countryside, constantly looking for the gaps that would let us easily into the next field. On many occasions one or other of them had no difficulty locating neat tunnels through thick hedges, thus considerably shortening the distance we had to walk.

Inland, Peter pointed out a stand of trees where Ballymacloud Farmhouse stood, close by the ruins of a small tower house. He told us that recently a cow had climbed up the circular stone stair of the castle and it had taken hours to get it back down again. I recalled a similar incident happening in a castle in Clare where it proved impossible to get the cow to descend, and the animal had to be slaughtered and butchered on the battlements!

After Ballymacloud, the river and Great Island across King's Channel came into view as we passed under a comfortable stone built house called Blenheim Lodge. On the riverbank near here we came across one of the most unusual sights I had seen in 120 miles of this coast: a hefty bull and his attendant bevy of cows, grazing in the company of a couple of goats, and a slender dark brown deer! The deer approached us with slender gracefulness and paused a few yards away sniffing the air, regarding us with big, trusting, liquid eyes. Peter put out his palm to the animal but it would not come any nearer. As we moved on, however, the deer followed us at a distance until we crossed a fence into another field.

On the hill above us now was another fine stone-built house, this one called simply Blenheim, as opposed to Blenheim Lodge. These two residences, together with another called Blenheim House further upriver, were built in the nineteenth century by the Sweetmans, a Waterford merchant family, using the same warm blend of stone walls and red brick window linings. Although each house is different in design, they are all finely proportioned and fit well into their rural settings. A replica of Blenheim House was apparently built by one of the family at Placentia, Newfoundland, and another at Poole in Dorset.

We now found ourselves being drawn away from the riverbank, following yet another inlet, the Knockboy Pill. A substantial acreage of low-lying land close to the river below us had been reclaimed by the construction of a dam, and we could see that we would have to skirt this to cross the Pill. Passing near Blenheim House, we walked along the edge of a wheatfield, searching for a

161

place where we could cross, and eventually found our way down through a tunnel of undergrowth where a tributary to the Pill cascaded down a rocky hill, and crossed where a substantial landfilling was in progress. Almost buried in the new ground we found a limekiln, suggesting that over a hundred years ago even the trickling Knockboy Pill was navigable to this point.

As we crossed the reclaimed land towards the dam, the sun broke out of the clouds and floodlit Slieve Coillte in Wexford, framed between the eastern end of Great Island and Faithlegge Hill. As quick as it came, the sun was gone, and the woods to the west vanished as a thick shower of rain hissed towards us. We made for the shelter of a ruined cottage, standing almost submerged under shrubs, forlorn in the middle of a field. Although the slated roof was holed in places, admitting great bunches of ripening elderberries, the place was otherwise dry, and we decided we might as well take the opportunity to have our lunch.

The little cottage had three rooms, timber floors and a fireplace in each room, which would have made it too luxurious to have been a smallholder's cottage in the nineteenth century. We wondered if it could have been a water bailiff's home, or indeed the cottage of the keeper of the nearby fish weir. There was no indication of how long it had been unoccupied, but the holes in the roof, together with the thick shrubs engulfing it, suggested that it

would not ward off nature much longer.

As soon as the rain had cleared, we crossed the reclaimed land to the dam and riverbank. Here the fish weir was obviously still very much in use; the nets forming the trap for the fish were in good condition, and there were signs along the shore of plenty of recent activity. Hanging on a post was an unusual net that Frank said may have been for catching eels.

We walked along the top of the dam for a while through eight-foot-high reeds. Inland we went again to skirt another inlet, passing by the back of St. Thomas's Church. Built in 1818, the tower of the church, topped with a weathervane and crowing cockerel, gives the hamlet roundabout the name 'The Brass Cock'. When the church became disused some years ago, the Church of Ireland authorities allowed a local badminton club use the building. While some of the parishioners were annoyed by the decision, it has meant that the building is being kept in good repair, and after seeing the numerous ruined churches along the coast it was a relief to find this one preserved and fulfiling a community need.

The riverbank below the church was a mass of tortoiseshell butterflies which had taken a liking to the nettles and some other, probably noxious, weed that covered the ground along the water's edge. They rose in a fluttering cloud as we approached, only to settle again as we passed. Among the tortoiseshells flocked a few red admirals with an identity crisis. Beyond the butterfly extravaganza, we turned inland briefly to get past the garden of a private house, and returned to the shore near a landing stage from which the car ferry to Little Island operates.

Little Island, named so to distinguish it from Great Island near the confluence of the Barrow, Nore and Suir, is about three quarters of a mile long and covers 300 acres. Geologically it is part of the northern, Kilkenny shore, and in former times the river between was said to have been periodically shallow enough to ford. All shipping to and from Waterford had to follow the deeper King's Channel to the south of the island, a tortuous twisting stretch that must have seen many sailing ships grounded in the mudbanks that line the shore. When vessels became larger and faster in the steamship era, the King's Channel constituted a stumbling block to the expansion and development of Waterford port, so it became necessary to dredge the north channel and blast its rocky link with Kilkenny to provide a proper navigable route upstream.

The Norman Fitzgeralds were granted the island in 1280, and held it until Nicholas Fitzgerald, the then lord of the manor was killed at the battle of the Boyne in 1690, commanding a section of Patrick Sarsfield's cavalry unit. The Fitzgerald estates were subsequently confiscated, but partially restored to the family later.

The Edward Fitzgerald who achieved fame by translating the epic *Rubáiyát of Omar Khayyám* was the son of a Fitzgerald of Little Island, and later in the nineteenth century during the time of the Great Famine, John Fitzgerald saved many in the Ballinakill area from emigration and probably worse by funding land drainage and reclamation of bogland at nearby Ballygunner.

Little Island has changed hands many times during the last sixty years, and through the 1930s and 1940s was the home of an Italian prince, Don Fernando d'Ardia Carrachiolo. Subsequent owners built extensive glasshouses, and farmed the land intensively. One had a spectacular way of crossing to the island; he drove an amphibious car, which looked in all respects like an ordinary car, and gave many onlookers and indeed some passengers who were unfamiliar with the situation a considerable fright, when he would drive without pause off the road, down the slipway and straight into the river! Now the island houses a luxury hotel, Waterford Castle, to which visitors gain access by helicopter or a car ferry that plies King's Channel from Ballinakill.

The 'Castle' in Waterford Castle is comparatively recent, the latest in many reconstructions and additions to the original Norman tower house built in the thirteenth century. Legend tells us that the old castle was linked by tunnel to Dunbrody Abbey, nearly a mile away across Waterford Harbour, and that the 'treasure' of Dunbrody is buried on the island. All castles have their ghost stories, and Waterford is no exception. One tells of a lady with long black hair with a very troubled look, who was seen frequently in the nineteenth century running up the main stairs as if being chased, and disappearing into the wall. During reconstruction work in 1905, an *oubliette* or secret chamber was discovered near the spot where she used to disappear. When it was opened up, a priest was brought in to bless it, and this particular ghost has not appeared since.

Turning upriver, we passed the back of Ballinakill House. Frank told me that some of the walls of the house are almost eight feet thick, suggesting it was built on the site of a fortified building, and that King James II is reputed to have spent the night there two days after the battle of the Boyne, before leaving Ireland via Passage for France.

We turned inland to cross a tributary stream, and found ourselves in a brand new housing estate, naked of trees, all white and pristine. Between this estate and the river, the developer had laid out a riverside walk. Peter said that Waterford Corporation was requiring all new developments along the riverbank to include such a path, so eventually the amenity may extend much of the way into town.

At the end of this particular length of pathway, however, our way upriver was interrupted by an elaborate refurbished house which looked as if it had been the original ferry-house for Little Island. Skirting inland around it, we regained the riverbank just under Belmont House, which was once the home of the late Charmaine Parkinson Hill, owner of the famous Cheltenham Gold Cup winner, Dawn Run.

On the riverbank here we found what appeared to be a salmon net, stretching out on floats forty yards into the river. I know little about the legality of such things, but we had seen quite a lot of evidence along the riverbank that fishing for salmon with nets was going on, and I doubt if any or all of it was legal.

Opposite Rathculliheen in County Kilkenny, a broad peninsula extends into the Suir where the river, split by Little Island, joins again, and heads south-west before straightening out and sweeping on up the quays of Waterford. The riverbank became narrower and more difficult to negotiate, but we eventually found, running parallel to the river and thirty feet above it, a very civilised pathway, following a linear wood that parallels the Suir for more than a half-mile. Here and there a strand of barbed wire indicated the end of one old demesne and the beginning of another, but the path carried on, wending its leafy way beneath Scots pines and magnificent beeches. Frank called me back at one stage, pointing upward through the canopy. Framed by a gap in the leaves was a heron, perched on a branch high above, seeming unaware of our passage below.

The only complaint I could have of what we found to be a marvellous riverside walk was the increase in sewage outlets to the river as we moved deeper into Waterford's suburbia. Although the weather was not particularly warm, the stench each time we passed one of these was very unpleasant.

Beside the pathway we came across an overgrown ornamental waterfall, cascading over a series of stone-built ledges and down into a decorative pond. The long neglect of the place was symbolised by moss-covered boulders and by a young sycamore tree which had established itself in the stonework, and was spectacularly bulging and bursting out, bringing the masonry slowly with it.

A track off the main path took us down briefly to the water's edge where we found a cast iron tower twelve feet high, painted red and white, and mounting a navigation light. On its side was cast the legend 'J. Moir 1888', which reminded me of the bollards along the disused quays of Dungarvan. In these days of planned obsolescence when almost everything is disposable, it is marvellous to come across manufactured objects such as this, the result of good materials and workmanship, having such a long and useful life.

A short distance further on, we found ourselves at the end of someone's garden, and for the first time since Youghal bridge, I had to retreat with profuse apologies when challenged by a flabbergasted householder who must have heard me shuffling around in the undergrowth! We were three miles from Waterford bridge.

We backtracked a little and found our way to the nearest public road, which luckily was only a hundred yards back from the river, and followed the road downhill through Newtown, towards the city.

In the late eighteenth century, when Waterford was at its most prosperous, wealthy merchants built the first houses in the Newtown area. During the nineteenth century, as a new middle class began to emerge in Waterford, they and people who wished

to move out of the centre of the town, built villas along Newtown Road, making it a pleasant, sought-after place to live. The only gap in development occurs at Newtown School, which is the oldest established school in Waterford. The strong Quaker community in the city purchased the property in 1797 and established the school, which has enjoyed a high reputation ever since. As we walked past, the green expanse of playing fields beside the school was peopled by figures dressed in brilliant white, playing cricket.

Before the Quakers founded a school here, the lands were owned by the Wyse family, which had held a prominent place in the annuals of Waterford since the Middle Ages. Being Catholics, they were banned for many years from taking part in the political life of the city, and lost much of their lands during Cromwell's time, so they turned their talents, very successfully, to commerce. In 1849 Thomas Wyse, a colleague of Daniel O'Connell in the struggle for Catholic Emancipation, was appointed ambassador to the newly established kingdom of Greece. His enlightened and progressive outlook is said to have helped influence the early development of the new regime.

On the opposite side of the road from the boundary wall of Newtown School a small limestone plaque mounted near a gateway tells that Field Marshal Lord Roberts, hero of Kandahar and winner of the Victoria Cross, lived here for a time. The 'here' meant originally Newtown Park, a fine late Georgian mansion overlooking the river. As a boy I passed this gateway every day on my way to and from school, by which time the demesne had been sold off for a number of house-sites, and Newtown Park was no longer visible from the road. I would often gaze at the legend on the plaque and puzzle at the tiny gate lodge, (now gone), that the 'here' seemed to refer to. One day, however, as I passed by, an old man whom I took to be gate lodge's occupant was pruning roses in the postage-stamp garden. To my amazement I saw he had only one leg; his empty trouser leg was neatly pinned up, and he moved about on crutches, his face shadowed mysteriously by his broad-brimmed hat. I decided that he must be Lord Roberts, nursing the wounds of his campaigns and fallen on hard times! For months after, I would always pause on the footpath, trying to pluck up courage to talk to the great man. I never did, and even long after it was scornfully proved to me by an older boy that this one-legged rose lover was not the Field Marshal who had died in 1914 my respect for, and wonder at this larger than life figure on crutches never waned.

Opposite the entrance gates to Newtown School, we passed the imposing facades and clock tower of De La Salle College, a secondary school and seminary. Built in the 1880s, it was the first large building in Waterford to have electric lighting installed during its construction.

Further on, opposite the People's Park, is Waterpark College, where I attended school from kindergarten to Leaving Certificate. Established by the Christian Brothers as a separate entity from Mount Sion in the 1920s, it was unusual in that it had tiny classes (my Leaving Certificate class numbered twelve), was fee-paying, and the boys togged out for rugby in the winter and hurling and cricket in the summer! Rugby was taken very seriously, and for such a small school Waterpark's teams were quite successful in the Munster Schoolboys Cup.

Beyond Waterpark we passed the premises of a builders' providers, the sad remnant of extensive timber yards and hardware stores that did a thriving trade in the 1950s. The quayside here was the scene of even greater industry when shipbuilding was carried out between 1847 and 1882. During this period the Neptune Iron Works built about forty steamships, the first of which, appropriately called the *S. S. Neptune*, inaugurated a regular service between London and St. Petersburg. She was the first steamship to enter the harbour of St. Petersburg, where she was greeted by a salute of guns and the Czar himself, who granted the vessel freedom from port dues forever! The Neptune Works also built Russia's first icebreaker, the 2,660 ton *S.S. Avoca*, and the *S.S. Una*, one of the first ships to pass through the Suez Canal.

Two hundred yards further on, we reached William Street and our destination for the day, a pub called the Three Shippes, where we discussed our day's trek over cool pints of Guinness. I was now within a few hundred yards of the old city of Waterford, and a mile-and-a-half short of my destination.

The following morning, the long and sometimes complicated cross-country treks behind me, I resumed my walk, setting off from William Street to enjoy the final stretch, a leisurely stroll through historic Waterford to the bridge.

William Street must have been named after one of the four British kings of that name. It seems strange today that the most popular of these, for a time anyway, was William of Orange, whose forces, fresh from their victory at the battle of the Boyne, invested the city with its Jacobite garrison in 1690. The city walls had been strengthened in preparation for a siege, but morale was very low after King James's defeat and departure for France. In addition, the Jacobites guns and ammunition were in poor condition.

There is evidence to suggest that the Williamite forces made use of the remains of a timber bridge crossing the Suir, a remnant of the earlier Cromwellian siege, to reach the south bank and surround the city. After four days of negotiation, the Jacobites capitulated, on condition they they and the remaining Catholic clergy in the city were given safe passage out. This peaceful transfer of power was further reinforced when William himself arrived at the city on 25 June, and gave strict orders to his forces that the citizens and their goods were not to be harmed. The citizenry must have been relieved and grateful to William; it was probably the first time in its history that the city had changed hands peacefully.

It is more likely, however, that William Street was named after the popular sailor-king William IV, whose short period on the throne, between 1830 and 1837, would probably coincide with the construction of the first houses on the street.

William Street becomes Lombard Street across one of Waterford's oldest bridges which spans St. John's Pill, in the old days a smelly, muddy tributary of the Suir that must have gathered much of its pollution at the gas works further upstream. Leaning over the worn limestone parapet, I could see that it was a much cleaner waterway now. I have always thought that, with the creation of a barrage dam near its outlet into the Suir, and a long-term improvement scheme, this winding waterway, which passes through the People's Park and along the picturesque Waterside, could become a major amenity and tourist attraction for the city.

Lombard Street is named after Peter Lombard, son of the wealthy sixteenth-century Waterford merchant. He must have spent only a short few years of his life in the city, for like many young Catholics of the time, he was sent abroad to receive an education. After studying at Louvain University, he was ordained to the priesthood. He became a very distinguished theologian, ultimately being appointed Archbishop of Armagh and Primate of Ireland by Pope Clement VIII, a post he held in absentia for twenty-five years until his death in Rome in 1625. There are two pubs in Lombard Street, and their names, The Royal Bar and Kings, are again reminders of Waterford's loyalist history.

Leaving the narrowness of Lombard Street, I walked out into the contrasting wide and sunny south-facing Mall, and with Waterford City's emblematic and rotund Reginald's Tower in view, I had reached the eastern boundary of old Norman Waterford.

In the mid-eighteenth century the Mall was a tree-lined pedestrian boulevard bounded by the old city walls on the west, where the fashionable citizenry strolled in summertime. Charles Smith, the historian, wrote of it in 1745: 'Nothing can be more agreeable than to see this shady walk crowded with the fair sex of the city, taking the air, enjoying the charms of a pleasant evening, and improving their healths: nor need I inform the reader that this city has long since been peculiarly celebrated for the beauties of its female inhabitants.'

At the river end of the Mall, opposite Reginald's Tower, was an extensive bowling green.

These amenities, however, disappeared in a rash of property development during the boom at the end of the eighteenth century. While most of the original city walls and the old Danish cathedral were demolished during this period, the city was enriched in return by the construction of many fine buildings, some of which adorn today's Mall.

On the western side, the grey limestone spire of the Church of Ireland cathedral, which Mark Girouard called 'the finest 18th-century ecclesiastical building in Ireland', forms the backdrop to the former Bishop's Palace, and the former Assembly Rooms and Theatre, now both housing offices of Waterford Corporation.

The original cathedral in Waterford was built during the late eleventh century, and was greatly added to in subsequent centuries. By 1773 the main building had fallen into disrepair and the Dublin architect, Thomas Ivory, recommended that it be rebuilt. In an unusual decision for the time, a Waterford architect was selected for the work. 'Honest' John Roberts, whose grandfather had come to Waterford from Wales, was born in 1712. His father, Thomas Roberts, was a builder-architect, and the young Roberts served his time in his father's firm before gaining some experience in England. On his return to Waterford he married Mary Sautelle, a member of a local Huguenot family, and the couple produced no less than twenty four children! This may explain the strange lack of examples of Roberts's early architectural work, because it is not until he was in his mid-sixties that he came to the fore as a designer, and from then until his death, he produced some of Waterford's finest buildings.

The cathedral is built over the crypt of the original cathedral and indeed is constructed substantially of the rubble from its demolition; when in the 1970s the walls were stripped for replastering, complete pieces of the original gothic columns could be seen built into the masonry.

On the terrace that slopes down from the Cathedral to the Mall

171

stands the old Bishop's Palace (c. 1740). Some say this building was also designed by Roberts, but I am inclined to agree with the theory that the German architect, Richard Castle, was responsible. He had already had episcopal clients by the 1730s, including the Bishop of Killala, for whom he designed a house in St. Stephen's Green in Dublin, and there are strong similarities between the Waterford building and his Westport House (1731). There was a time in the 1970s when this fine building might have been demolished to make way for a modern office block, like the ESB building across the road. Sanity prevailed, however, and its future is now secure.

Between the Bishop's Palace and Reginald's Tower on the street front stands the Town Hall, which has been a social and cultural centre for two hundred years. Designed as a playhouse and assembly rooms by Roberts

and built in 1787, the New Rooms, as they were called at that time, served as the city's premier venue for banquets, masquerades, plays and musical evenings. The consortium of Waterford citizens who built the New Rooms were given a 999-year lease by the Corporation for a shilling a year, on condition that the Mayor and Corporation could have the use of the building for public occasions and receptions. In one of its first official uses, the Corporation sumptuously decorated the banqueting hall to entertain Crown Prince William, later to become King William IV, to a ceremonial breakfast on his visit to the city.

On the rising tide of prosperity that flooded Waterford in the late eighteenth century, the city's merchant classes soon made the place their own, with hardly a week going by during the 'season' without a ball or masquerade being held, some of which caused such traffic jams that instructions for the smooth movement of carriages and sedan chairs had to be given in the local newspapers. The finely preserved theatre is today home to the Waterford Light Opera Festival, held every autumn, when musical societies from all over the British Isles come to Waterford to compete and entertain.

Leaving the Town Hall behind, I walked back down the Mall towards the river and Waterford's Quay. Dominating the river here today, as it has done for many centuries, is Reginald's Tower. The present structure is of indeterminate age; certainly the top third looks to have been built at a different period to the bottom two-thirds, and it is very possible that the building was substantially rebuilt many times, over the nine centuries it is said to have stood here. It houses what was up to recently Waterford's only museum, displaying Royal Charters, the ceremonial swords of Kings John and Henry VII, and old maps of the city, but curiously, it was a Saturday when I passed and it was not open.

The Suir is nearly 300 metres wide at this point, a broad, strongly flowing river that has been the lifeblood of this city since its foundation by Scandinavian settlers in the ninth century. As one rounds Reginald's Tower on to Waterford's Quay, the jumble of dock buildings and gigantic blue container cranes is all that can be seen initially, and one wonders where is this 'noblest quay in Europe', claimed by historian Mark Girouard. My approach to Waterford unfortunately was the wrong way for one who wanted to experience this noble quay, best seen from the Kilkenny side of the river, preferably on high ground. From there, the number and scale of the houses and shops fronting onto the Suir far outshine the more recent industrial additions.

The river Suir rises in the Devil's Bit mountains, six miles north-west of the town of Templemore; the old annals say it began to flow together with the Barrow and Nore on the night that King Conn of the Hundred Battles was born. Its broad sheltered reach at Waterford, overlooked by a small defensible promontory behind Reginald's Tower, obviously appealed to the Scandinavian seafarers, who would have used the place as a winter base, and eventually, tired of the hard life at sea, settled and established a trading post. Before long the prosperity of the new Vethrafjorthr (the fiord of Odin, father of the Norse gods) grew, as its inhabitants traded with the indigenous population and passing shipping. By the twelfth century, Waterford was a fortified city with its own bishop and a mixed population of Vikings and native Irish. When the Normans came in 1170, it suffered the first of many major sieges, ending with a Norman victory and the slaughter of its defenders.

For the next 700 years, Waterford remained intensely loyal to the English Crown, earning from King Henry VII the motto 'Urbs Intacta Manet Waterfordia' for its violent rejection of royal pretenders.

The port here was for a long period one of the chief ports of the country, earning it the name Waterford of the Ships. At the height of its prosperity towards the end of the eighteenth century, it merited the stationing of an impressive naval force, including a frigate and two cutters. Frigates were the next class of ship below a ship-of-the-line or battleship, had two decks carrying anything from 20 to 50 guns, while cutters had a crew of 40 and carried up to 17 guns.

In addition to the revenue provided by the river, it has often provided entertainment for the populace. Regattas have always been popular here due to the grandstand view provided by the Quay. Organised boat races began in the eighteenth century, with the City Corporation giving silver cups to the winners. A contemporary account of a regatta day refers to 'a prodigious concourse' of spectators, who 'swarmed like bees' along the Quay, and filled the windows of every house overlooking the river. The population were entertained to a firework display on the night of the regatta, while a military band located on the Corporation Barge played music as it was rowed up and down the Quay.

The combination of the length of Waterford's Quay and the scale of the buildings that line it makes it unique; it is a feature remarked upon by most visitors down the centuries. Charles Smith in 1745 claimed it 'rather exceeds the most celebrated in Europe', while Arthur Young thirty years later stated 'The finest object in this city is the quay, which is unrivalled by any I have seen; it is an English mile long; the buildings on it are only common houses, but the river near a mile over, flows up to the town in one noble reach, and the opposite shore a bold hill, which rises immediately from the water to a height that renders the whole magnificent.' William Makepeace Thackeray, not unused to being less than complimentary to all things Irish, reported after his visit: 'The view of the town from the bridge and the heights above it is very imposing; as is the river both ways. Very large vessels sail up almost to the doors of the houses, and the quays are flanked by tall red warehouses, that look at a little distance as if a world of business might be doing within them.'

Another visitor in 1836 found Waterford a 'dark dirty, mean-looking place, but improves on advancing towards the fine quay . . .', but when he stayed overnight in a hotel on the quay, his attitude changed when he was rudely awakened by 'the intolerable noise of the grunting and squeaking of multitudes of pigs that are driven down the Quay at an early hour . . .' *Murray's Guide* thirty years later confesses that Waterford 'generally speaking, has an ancient and fishlike smell, mixed up with an odour of butter and pigs.'!

But for a few exceptions, the Quay has retained its pleasant scale to the present, although there is nothing quaint about the operation of a modern port, and the buildings and paraphernalia involved have changed, at least temporarily, the ambience of the place. A dock strike that spanned the 1970s and 1980s, reducing the port to a container terminal, may be looked upon in years to come as saving what remained of the old quays from destructive development, for when attitudes to conservation changed in the 1980s, there was still plenty left in Waterford to conserve.

The names of the streets off the Quay could be used as headings in a history lesson about the city. Greyfriars, leading up to Christchurch Cathedral, passes the ruins of a Franciscan church founded in 1240. Many prominent Waterford citizens of the sixteenth, seventeenth and eighteenth centuries are buried in the nave of the church, as is Sir Neal O'Neille, friend and lieutenant of King James II, who died at Waterford after being mortally wounded at the battle of the Boyne.

A more modern church in Greyfriars has been converted to a Heritage Centre, where the best of the artefacts from recent archaeological excavations in Waterford are displayed. Waterford's strong links with Europe since its foundation as a trading port are evidenced by the substantial finds of exquisite richly glazed pottery from medieval France, Germany, Britain and Italy. A seven-foot high 3D collage depicting the layering exposed in an excavation, from the modern tarmac surface down through brick, rubble and bones to Viking timbers lying on undisturbed boulder clay, gives a marvellous insight into the science of archaeology.

Henrietta Street is probably named after the wife of Charles I, Henrietta Maria. Further up, past the General Post Office, the hardware emporium of John Hearnes is one of the last of the old style shops on the Quay. While almost all others have by now fancy floor finishes of vinyl or carpet, John Hearnes's floor remains the serviceable bare scrubbed timber it has been for donkey's years. The place is an Aladdin's cave of hardware, stacked against the wall, hanging from the ceiling, or in vast areas of pigeon holes or drawers lining the walls. However, the most impressive thing about John Hearnes is the quality of service that can be expected. Any member of the staff will courteously devote fifteen or twenty minutes, or as long as it takes, to locate an exact match for an old broken screw of obscure and non-metric make, wrap it in a strong brown paper bag, and hand you back change out of ten pence, wishing you 'Good Luck, now!'

Conduit Lane, just beyond John Hearnes, recalls the laying in the sixteenth century of an extensive city water supply using pipes make of elm wood. The network was extended down this street to the Quay to supply the ships moored in the river.

Barronstrand Street harks back to the time when outside the city walls, below a tower erected by the Dane, Turgesius, there was a sandy inlet owned by someone called Barron.

Opposite Barronstrand Street on the Quay stands that other symbol of Waterford, the gothic spire-like Clock Tower. Designed by an architect named Tarrant, it was erected in 1861 at a cost of £200. Its three-and-a-half feet diameter clocks were intended to be visible from anywhere in the main port area, but the forest of high masts and rigging still carried by most ships at the time it was built prevented this. I crossed the street and walked around the tower, as if seeing it for the first time, and was surprised that I had not noticed its finer qualities before. It really is an excellent piece of street architecture, its gothic design using a careful blend of grey limestone and sandy granite. I discovered that the tower served users of the Quay in other ways besides giving the time. On three sides there are drinking fountains, with finely carved granite surrounds and washbasins, overlooked by carved Viking-like faces in limestone. At ground level I was amused to find that the dog population is similarly catered for, their drinking water issuing from tiny dog's-head gargoyles.

Gladstone Street is named for the nineteenth-century British prime minister, and leads up to one of Waterford's finest town-houses, now occupied by the Chamber of Commerce. John Roberts designed the building for a wealthy merchant in the 1780s, and although the facade was remodelled in Victorian times, the entrance door, the fine internal plasterwork and the exceptional oval staircase are all original, and further evidence of Roberts's considerable talents.

At Hanover Street some of the last of the great warehouses of Waterford's prosperous trading era can be seen, sombre five-storey stone and brick structures.

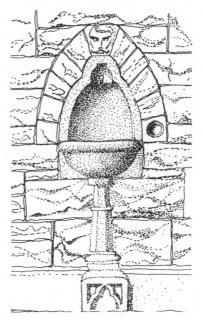

I was a few hundred yards from Waterford bridge when the open countryside to the west of the city came into view, domi-nated by the rounded Slieve na mBan. The 'new' bridge, com-pleted in the late 1980s after many delays and one major hold-up when half of the centre section fell into the river, was now beginning to look like it had always been there.

Until the first proper bridge was build here in 1794, Waterford city, and indeed much of the eastern county, might as well have been an off-shore island. It was an isolated city state, as much in touch with

Bristol and Cadiz as it was with Dublin. Direct contact with the rest of Ireland was in the hands of a family called Roche, a member of which had been granted the valuable ferry rights for his assistance to the besieged city of Derry in 1689. Waterford's golden age in the late eighteenth century, the remaining symbols of which include John Roberts's buildings, was marked by the determination of some of its prominent citizens to have the city realise its full economic potential, to climb out of the Middle Ages and become integrated with the rest of Ireland. A substantial bridge spanning the Suir was for them the keystone of this policy.

The financing of the project was elaborate and complex, especially when it came to compensating for the ferry rights, but the result was a fine forty-foot wide structure in American oak, erected in ten months and opened in January 1794.

The bridge was from the outset a toll bridge, and a lucrative investment for those citizens who had become financially involved in the project. By the mid-nineteenth century, however, public outcry about the tolls on Old Timbertoes, as the bridge became known, led to them being reduced to a halfpenny for a pedestrian and '2 shillings and 6 pence for every Coach, Breslin, Calash, Chariot, Chaise or Chair drawn by six or more horses or beasts of burden'. Funeral processions were free, which meant that people being buried on the far side of the river were assured of a good send off!

In 1907 the Corporation of Waterford, which must have had a good year, purchased the bridge for £63,000. After a night of celebrations, to the sound of ships' sirens, firecrackers and church bells, the gates were opened at midnight on December 31 and almost the entire population of the city followed the mayor across the Suir free of charge.

A new reinforced concrete bridge, constructed to replace the ageing Timbertoes, was opened in February 1913, and it lasted seventy years before being replaced by the present structure.

It was quite an anticlimax to reach the bridge, and come to the end of a journey I had dreamed about and planned during a dark Dublin winter. As I stood looking out over the waters of the olive green Suir flowing purposefully towards the sea, trying in vain to conjure up some appropriate ending for this narrative, a grey black cloud front drifted down from Slieve na mBan and it started to rain. I gave up all literary pretensions and crossed the road to have a celebratory drink in the Crystal Bar.